THE COMPLETE DBT AND CBT WORKBOOK FOR TEENS

CLAIM YOUR EMOTIONS AND BUILD RESILIENCE

CATHERINE L. ABBOTT

© **Copyright 2023 - All rights reserved.**

The content contained within this book may not be reproduced, duplicated or transmitted without direct written permission from the author or the publisher.

Under no circumstances will any blame or legal responsibility be held against the publisher, or author, for any damages, reparation, or monetary loss due to the information contained within this book, either directly or indirectly.

Cover Design Attribution:

The image used on the cover of this book is attributed to JCOMP on Freepik. Thank you for the amazing design.

Legal Notice:

This book is copyright protected. It is only for personal use. You cannot amend, distribute, sell, use, quote or paraphrase any part, or the content within this book, without the consent of the author or publisher.

Disclaimer Notice:

Please note the information contained within this document is for educational and entertainment purposes only. All effort has been executed to present accurate, up to date, reliable, complete information. No warranties of any kind are declared or implied. Readers acknowledge that the author is not engaged in the rendering of legal, financial, medical or professional advice. The content within this book has been derived from various sources. Please consult a licensed professional before attempting any techniques outlined in this book.

By reading this document, the reader agrees that under no circumstances is the author responsible for any losses, direct or indirect, that are incurred as a result of the use of the information contained within this document, including, but not limited to, errors, omissions, or inaccuracies.

CONTENTS

Introduction	7
1. UNDERSTANDING EMOTIONS	11
The Positive Twist	14
The Teenage Emotional Rollercoaster	15
The Power of Behavioral Therapy	18
2. GETTING TO KNOW YOURSELF	23
Exploring Yourself	24
Practicing Mindfulness	28
Emotional Awareness	32
3. CONNECTING YOUR THOUGHTS TO YOUR FEELINGS AND BEHAVIORS	35
Understanding Thoughts, Feelings, and Behaviors	36
The ABC Model	38
Challenging Negative Thoughts	44
4. DISTRESS TOLERANCE SKILLS	49
Learning to Self-Soothe	50
Look at the Pros and Cons	52
STOP Technique	53
Radical Acceptance	55
5. EMOTIONAL REGULATION SKILLS	57
Building Your Emotion Regulation Toolkit	60
Opposite Action	61
Coping Ahead	63
Checking the Facts	65
Ride the Wave	67
Find Enjoyment in Life	69

6. INTERPERSONAL EFFECTIVENESS
   SKILLS ... 71
   Effective Communication ... 72
   DEAR MAN Technique ... 78
   Setting Boundaries ... 80

7. MIND-BODY CONNECTION ... 85
   Taking Care of Your Physical Well-Being ... 86
   Relaxation Techniques ... 91

8. COPING WITH SPECIFIC EMOTIONS ... 99
   Managing Your Anger ... 100
   Dealing With Anxiety ... 103
   Overcoming Depression ... 107

9. BUILDING RESILIENCE ... 113
   Cultivating Resilience ... 114
   Creating a Growth Mindset ... 118
   Developing a Support System ... 122

10. PUTTING IT ALL TOGETHER ... 127
    Creating a Personalized Plan ... 128
    Setting Goals ... 130
    Maintaining Progress ... 134

11. LOOKING AHEAD ... 137
    Celebrate Your Progress ... 138
    Develop Lifelong Skills ... 139

    Conclusion ... 145
    References ... 147

INTRODUCTION

Being a teenager and dealing with the big emotions, changes, stress, and anxiety that come with it may arguably be one of the most difficult times of your life so far. You may feel like nobody understands you or doesn't even try to know what you're going through. How could they if, far too often, you don't even understand yourself or the intense feelings that keep bubbling inside of you?

If that's not enough, your body is going through many physical changes, some of them expected, while others seem to be so out of the blue that they feel like a knock to the stomach. You may even feel embarrassed by some of these changes, especially when your development is at a different pace (either faster or slower) than that of your peers. Your friends may also start to pressure you to do things or behave in ways that are uncharacteristic of you, and saying "no" to them brings about fears of social isolation and ridicule.

Apart from the changes to your body, your life is going through changes. Your time at school is nearing its end, and soon, you'll need to make decisions that will affect the rest of your life. Unless you know what you want to do in the future (and let's face it, most teenagers don't for sure), this can add an enormous amount of stress to your life. This stress can make it even more difficult to make decisions or focus on your schoolwork. Add to this the fact that you'll likely struggle more with your schoolwork, as it will not only become more difficult but also increase in quantity.

Then, there is the big range of hormones that are rushing through your body. Many of these hormones are new to you, and not only will your physical body have to learn to adjust to having these hormones, but you will also need to learn to cope with them on a mental and emotional level as well.

This may make you feel like shutting yourself in your room, switching off the lights, and pulling the blankets over your head in the hopes that the world will forget about your existence. But, regardless of how dark your life may seem right now, you need to realize that you're most definitely not alone. The challenges that teenagers face on a daily basis affect all adolescents, some just on a deeper and more psychological level. This is evident in studies that show that one in three teenagers struggles with anxiety disorder (*Any anxiety disorder*, n.d.).

Luckily, you can learn to manage your anxiety, stress, and intense emotions more effectively. This will help you not only cope with the everyday challenges you face but also give you the confidence you need to make important decisions. The techniques taught in behavioral therapy, both dialectical behavior therapy (DBT) and cognitive behavioral therapy (CBT), can help you find the inner peace you so deeply desire and place you in a position where you can find happiness and live your best life.

As a parent, I understand the struggles that you face. My son went through the same struggles that you're dealing with today. I was determined to help my child cope with his difficulties, and I saw the amazing effects that DBT and CBT can have on a teenager's life. This has ignited a passion within me to help other teenagers surmount the challenges that come with this stage of their lives. Apart from working with others on a one-on-one basis, I started to speak at community events and have written numerous books to share my knowledge.

Now, I want to help you gain a better understanding of what you're going through so that you can overcome these difficulties and become the happy, thriving adult you were meant to be.

1

UNDERSTANDING EMOTIONS

Before you continue reading this book and work on overcoming your challenges, take a few minutes to think about what you're feeling right now. Are you curious about what you'll learn? Are you hopeful about improving your future? Or perhaps you are scared of the future and fear that you won't ever cope with your challenges.

All of these—hope, curiosity, happiness, and fear—are emotions that are not only absolutely natural to experience but also make us human. Emotions are more than just feelings. They help us determine what we are thinking, what we want in life, and how we want to respond.

We experience our first emotions as infants. Think of a young baby's laughter or crying to get the attention of their caregivers. Emotions are the only way for young babies to communicate with others and make sure their needs are met. It's also their first way of building bonds with other people.

As we grow up, we learn that these feelings have names. In many cases, this is done in the form of nursery songs that encourage kids to clap their hands if they are happy. Young children are taught about basic emotions such as happy, sad, angry, or scared, and over time, emotional awareness is created.

However, all of this early learning is often thrown out the window when we become teenagers. This is when our emotions often start to run rampant with us. Not only are we suddenly experiencing new and different emotions—often going from being happy to sad to angry in a few minutes' time—but these emotions are also suddenly a lot more intense than ever before. When we are unable to control our feelings effectively, it can result in severe emotional outbursts that can lead to conflict and potentially damage our relationships with others.

Some people are naturally more in touch with their emotions and, as a result, can manage their feelings more effectively. But, for most of us, emotional awareness and regulation take practice and a continuous effort to allow ourselves to feel our emotions and then decide how we choose to respond to them.

While we can go into great detail on the complexity of emotions, there are five things that are absolutely vital to know and remember:

- Having emotions is absolutely natural and even healthy.
- Experiencing strong emotions doesn't make you a bad person.
- Emotions will always come and go. While some will last for only a few seconds, others can linger for a long time.
- Emotions can be experienced in a variety of intensities, ranging from mild to extremely intense.
- No emotion is good or bad. The negativity that's often associated with specific emotions is a result of our reactions to these feelings.

Managing your emotions is, therefore, all about controlling your behavior. Once you can do this, you'll soon understand that even the typical negative emotions, such as anger or jealousy, can be positive. It's all about your own perception of these feelings and the power you allow them to have in your life.

THE POSITIVE TWIST

Let's take a deeper look at the positivity that surrounds all feelings. Some emotions may seem obviously positive, such as being happy, confident, cheerful, interested, grateful, or loving. However, these don't necessarily have to mean something good. The right amount of confidence is fantastic, but having too little or too much can have many negative effects on your life and your ability to thrive. Similarly, we all want to feel loved, but too much love can feel suffocating.

On the flip side, emotions that are typically perceived as negative can actually have a positive effect on your life. For example, anger can teach you what you don't want in your life and what boundaries you should set, and fear can help you make quick decisions that can, in severe circumstances, actually save your life.

It's also impossible to avoid experiencing the types of emotions that are typically regarded as negative, such as jealousy, regret, or shame. It's inevitable that, at some point in your life, you will experience situations that will evoke these feelings in you. If you try to avoid them, you'll only end up judging yourself for having these difficult feelings and holding on to them for much longer than you have to, which will ultimately have a negative effect on your physical, mental, and emotional health.

This is why it's so important that you learn how to manage them and choose how you would like to behave instead of allowing these so-called negative emotions (I prefer calling them unhelpful emotions) to take control of your life. In later chapters, we'll discuss various techniques and exercises that you can use to improve your ability to regulate your emotions by recognizing, respecting, and accepting your feelings and then allowing yourself to move on from them.

THE TEENAGE EMOTIONAL ROLLERCOASTER

Teenagers generally experience intense emotions and mood swings ranging from extreme highs to the lowest of lows. This doesn't make you weird in any way; it simply makes you a typical teenager who's developing into an adult. The intensity of your emotions and your subsequent behavior do, however, depend on your individual circumstances and your ability to adjust your behavior.

It's impossible to pinpoint just one reason why teenagers often experience extreme emotional highs and lows, as they are usually caused by a combination of these three factors:

- **Physical factors**: As we've mentioned, teenagers go through many different physical changes. Your body is changing and developing into that of an adult. This can make you self-conscious and increase your need for privacy. Your interests are changing, which often brings about changes in your sleeping patterns. Whereas as a young child or preteen you likely had strict bedtimes, your interests might result in these bedtimes changing, causing you to have less time to sleep. This can severely impact your mood. Your eating habits might also have changed as you became more conscious of your body and nutrition. Changing your diet can result in the release of many different hormones in your body, which may affect your mood.
- **Brain factors**: A person's brain continues to change until well into their 20s. The last section of the brain to develop, the prefrontal cortex, typically only reaches maturity around the age of 25. This is the part of the brain that's responsible for regulating emotions, so even though you'll experience more varied and

intense emotions during adolescence, your brain may be physically unable to fully manage them. Then, there is the rush of hormones that your body is starting to release. One of the biggest changes from pre-teen to teenager is the release of sex hormones, which not only results in physical changes in the body but also creates romantic and sexual feelings, which can be extremely confusing.

- **Social and emotional factors**: As you get older, your priorities change, and your friends will become more important. This means that you'll not only want to spend more time with your friends, but you'll also be more susceptible to the effects of peer pressure. This can lead to a lot of tension, which can result in many strong emotions. Teenagers typically also start to test their independence from their parents and want to do more things by themselves. This can be an emotional process: You may not be physically, emotionally, or mentally ready for the pressures that come with independence, or your parents may be unwilling to allow you the level of independence that you desire.

The reasons for your big emotions may not be limited to these three factors. As we've already mentioned, your schoolwork and stress over your future can also cause emotional ups and downs. Or, your biggest emotional stressor may be something completely different, such as moving to a new house or problems in your family. Whatever the cause of your big emotions may be, always remember that it's not only normal to have big emotions but also that most teenagers struggle with managing their feelings.

THE POWER OF BEHAVIORAL THERAPY

Even the most intense and unhelpful emotions can lose their power if you're able to adjust how you respond to them. This is where behavioral therapies such as DBT and CBT can be so valuable, as they will help you calm down, adjust your expectations, and then choose how you want to respond to these feelings.

Behavioral therapy is built on the premise that all behaviors are learned, whether consciously or subconsciously, and just like you've learned to behave in a problematic way, you can learn to respond to your challenges in a more positive or helpful way.

Cognitive Behavioral Therapy

CBT is one of the most common types of psychotherapy, or talk therapy, where you learn to identify your unhelpful thought patterns that result in negative behaviors or emotions. It helps you not only understand the negative thoughts you may have and how this can affect your mental and emotional well-being but also to replace these thoughts and subsequent behaviors with more desirable ones. Some of the most common techniques used in CBT include:

- **Identifying negative or limiting thoughts**: Our emotions are driven by the thoughts that we have, and in many cases, the negative thoughts that are controlling our lives are baseless. By practicing introspection and looking for specific evidence to back our thoughts, we can learn to differentiate between the truth and fictional negative thoughts.
- **Practicing new skills**: In CBT, you're taught skills that you can immediately implement in your life. These include new coping techniques.
- **Setting goals**: When you're trying to improve your life, it's important that you set realistic and achievable goals. Through CBT, you'll learn how to differentiate between short- and long-term goals and how to focus not only on your desired outcomes but on the process as a whole.
- **Improved problem-solving**: Experiencing problems can result in intense emotions, especially when you struggle with finding

solutions to your problems. Following CBT's five steps for problem-solving can make this easier for you:

- Identify the problem.
- Create a list of possible solutions.
- Consider the pros and cons of each solution.
- Decide which solution to implement.
- Evaluate the solution after implementation.
- **Monitoring yourself**: There may be times when you get so overwhelmed by the intense emotions that you have that you struggle to solve your problems or think of more helpful ways to behave. In these cases, CBT teaches you to practice self-monitoring, where you track your own symptoms, emotions, thoughts, behaviors, and experiences to understand and manage your emotions more effectively.

Dialectical Behavior Therapy

The other form of behavioral therapy that we'll discuss in this book is DBT. This is a modified type of CBT, and while it was originally intended to treat mental health conditions such as borderline personality disorder, it has proven to be extremely effective in not only managing other mental health conditions but also reducing stress and anxiety, improving your relationships with others, and regulating your emotions more effectively. It's built on four pillars:

- **Mindfulness**: This is about focusing on what is currently happening in your life and your body—including your thoughts, feelings, impulses, and sensations—instead of worrying over what might happen in the future. It's about accepting yourself and your current circumstances without judgment and slowing down your thoughts so that you can calmly find the solutions that you seek.
- **Distress tolerance**: This aspect of DBT helps you in times of crisis or intense emotions, as the techniques help you cope with the challenges you face with a longer-term outlook in mind.
- **Interpersonal effectiveness**: If you don't work on building proper relationships with others, it can result in emotional difficulty and stress. This pillar of DBT aims to help you build healthier relationships with others by respecting yourself and others and becoming more assertive in your communication.
- **Emotional regulation**: When you regulate your emotions, you learn to identify and accept your emotions, allow yourself to feel these feelings,

and then decide how you want to respond to these powerful feelings.

Now that you have a better understanding of emotions and the behavioral therapies that we'll discuss in this book, let's turn our attention to you and help you understand what you're struggling with.

2

GETTING TO KNOW YOURSELF

How well do you know yourself? I'm not just referring to your name or the qualities and thoughts that you comfortably share with others, but also the innermost you that you keep hidden from others and sometimes even yourself. This is the deepest level of your being and includes the thoughts that you may be too scared to admit having, the emotions you may desperately try to avoid, your dreams (even those that seem to be completely unrealistic), and your personal values.

Getting to know your true self means becoming aware of all these attributes, accepting that they all add together to make you a whole person, and allowing yourself to be truly yourself. It's about differentiating between the person that others believe you are and who you, in your heart and subconscious mind, know you are.

Apart from discovering who you truly are, getting to know yourself will help you identify things that might be missing from your life, which will help you set the necessary goals to improve your life.

EXPLORING YOURSELF

The first step in your journey of self-discovery should be to examine yourself and your life so that you can identify your values and strengths and find out who you are and what might be missing from your life. There are many different ways in which you can explore yourself, such as:

Visualize your future self: Take some time to think about where you'd like to be in the future. What does this best version of yourself look like? What are you doing? Who do you surround yourself with? What makes you happy? What makes me proud?

Reflect on your past self: Now, take some time to think about your past. Start by thinking of a time you felt really bad about yourself. What happened at that moment to make you feel that way? What emotions were you feeling? What thoughts did you have? How did you behave? Once you're done reflecting on a negative version of yourself, think about a time when you were at your happiest. What led to this happiness? Who contributed to these positive feelings? What other emotions did you experience? What thoughts consume your mind? How did you behave?

Explore your passions: Take some time to think about the things that you're passionate about. These are the things that make you happy by simply thinking about them and that you look forward to doing. Make a list of your passions and do something on this list as often as you can, especially when you're feeling down.

Try something new: If you don't have any specific passions yet or want to develop new ones, you should make a habit of trying new things. This can be learning a new skill, going to places you've never been before, or adopting a new hobby. The more you expose yourself to new things, the easier it will be to discover new passions and get to know yourself.

Zooming in on your skills: As you're learning new skills or discovering your passions, you'll hone in on what you can do. Make lists of the things you do well and see how you can use these skills more often.

Consider your values: Your personal values are the aspects of your life or qualities of your personality that you find most important. The values that you find to be most meaningful will help you uncover your true self and realize how you expect others to behave. Good values can include honesty, loyalty, compassion, courage, and kindness.

Ask questions: Self-discovery will often require you to ask specific questions to try to understand your behavior and determine how you'd like it to change in the future. Be honest when you ask yourself questions, and remember that this isn't done to try to impress others but rather to improve yourself. A general rule of thumb is that when you struggle to answer a specific question, it may be an indication that change is needed in your life. Typical questions you can ask yourself include:

- Why do I do the things I do?
- What makes me excited?
- What makes me upset?
- What might be missing in my life?
- What are the consequences of my decisions?
- What changes do I want to make?

Keeping a journal: Journaling about your daily life, your triumphs, and your struggles can provide you with valuable insights into what you want in life and what you find important. Through self-reflection, you can identify unhelpful behavioral patterns or how specific situations ignite intense emotions within you. Always remember that your journal can be as private as you want it to be. If you want to share your journal with others, you can, but if you want to keep your innermost thoughts private, you never have to show them to anyone.

Talk to someone: There may be times when you struggle to identify your struggles or find better ways to improve your behavior, limit your unhelpful thoughts, and regulate your intense emotions. It can then be helpful to talk to someone you trust and ask for their advice. This can be a friend or an adult, such as your parents, caregivers, teachers, or doctor. Since these people will have a different point of view from yours, they may give insights into your problem that you haven't considered yet.

Self-discovery should be seen as an ongoing process and not a once-off event. As you grow as a person, your values and strengths may change, which may require you to take a different approach to solving your problems. By practicing self-discovery frequently, you'll stay aware of your true self and be able to immediately identify things that are missing from your life.

The process of exploring yourself will look different for everyone, and the techniques that work for one person might not work for the next. For this reason, I encourage you to try all of the techniques listed here. After trying them, you'll discover which ones work best for you.

PRACTICING MINDFULNESS

Mindfulness is the practice of being fully present in the moment and accepting yourself without judgment while you focus on your senses and breathing. It's about focusing only on your current reality without regrets over past mistakes or worries about the future. It also gives you a moment to calm your thoughts and feelings so that you can decide how you want to respond to your challenges in a more helpful way.

There are many ways to practice mindfulness in your daily life, with the most popular form being meditation. This is an ancient Buddhist practice that has since been adopted by people all around the world. You don't have to be religious or spiritual to practice mindful meditation. Also, don't be fooled by how meditation is often stereotypically portrayed in movies—you don't have to sit in the lotus position with your hands facing upward while you chant something like "Ohm!"

Mindful meditation is extremely easy to do. Simply follow these basic steps, but feel free to adjust them as you get more comfortable with this practice:

1. Sit somewhere comfortable. This can be on the floor, on a chair, or on the bed. Where and how you sit aren't as important as feeling at ease. If you're sitting on a chair, let your feet touch the ground with your arms falling to your sides and your hands resting either on your lap or on the ground on either side of you.
2. Make sure you turn off all distractions. Put your phone on silent and switch the TV off. If you want to play calming music while you meditate, that's okay as long as the music doesn't distract you.
3. Take a few deep breaths and allow your breathing to settle into a calming rhythm. We'll discuss a few deep breathing exercises in Chapter 7, but the most important is to inhale through your nose and exhale through your mouth by pursing your lips. Focus only on your breathing.
4. Once your breathing has settled into a deep rhythm, you can do a quick sensory check by focusing on what you're feeling, seeing, hearing, smelling, and tasting. If this is too distracting for you, you can simply keep your focus on your breathing with closed eyes.
5. Spend a few minutes in this state of relaxation with your focus only on the air filling and

exiting your body. It's inevitable for thoughts to enter your mind. When this happens, simply accept your thoughts and feelings without any judgment and return your focus to your breathing.
6. When you're done, you can close the session by simply doing a deep breathing technique. If you want, you can repeat a positive affirmation, such as "I'm calm, I'm powerful, I'm important, and I'm capable."

You can decide how long you want to meditate. The general rule of thumb is to meditate for between 5–10 minutes daily, but you can do this for longer or more often if you want. If you decide on a timeframe for your meditation session, it can be helpful to set a timer to let you know when this time is finished, especially if you have a very busy schedule or want to meditate before studying for an exam. This way, you can focus only on being mindful without wondering how long you've been busy or fearing that you'll spend too much time meditating.

Meditation is only one of the many ways in which you can practice mindfulness. You can also do it while you're busy with your chores, such as cleaning the house, working in the garden, going for a walk, or taking a bath. Simply focus on the specific task you're busy with and how you're feeling at that specific moment. If your mind drifts to your past mistakes or future worries, simply bring it back to the present. Even just deciding to complete only one task at a time instead of trying to multitask can bring some level of mindfulness.

When you start with this practice, you may have to make a concerted effort to spend a few minutes daily in a state of mindfulness; this practice doesn't come naturally to everyone. But the more you do it, the easier it will be to find a place of mindfulness. Eventually, you'll even be able to do a super quick meditation session in the middle of the classroom, on the sports field, or even in a crowded mall.

There are also many applications you can download onto your phone that will guide you to becoming more mindful. This is especially helpful if you struggle with calming your racing thoughts to focus only on the present. If you struggle with this practice, be kind to yourself and show yourself the same compassion you would show a close friend. As long as you don't give up and continue trying to find a place of inner peace, you will get there.

EMOTIONAL AWARENESS

Increasing your awareness of your emotions is another important aspect of getting to know yourself, as this will help you identify and label the various emotions you experience on a daily basis. Emotional awareness is also the first step in improving your emotional regulation, which we'll discuss in more detail in Chapter 5. It will also help you get to know and accept yourself.

You can start to increase your emotional awareness by following these three steps:

1. **Name your feelings**: When you experience a strong emotion, try your best to name it. By doing this, you remind yourself that what you're feeling is nothing more than an emotion and that if you choose not to respond to it, the intensity of this feeling will gradually and naturally decrease. While you're naming your emotion, think about the situation in which you experienced it. Are you feeling nervous before you take an exam? Do you feel excited when your crush gives you attention? Maybe you're feeling relaxed when you listen to calming music. Put as much context behind your emotions as you can.

2. **Rate your emotions**: Once you know what you're feeling, you can rate the intensity of these emotions. I recommend you rate them on a scale of 1–10, where 1 is the mildest form of the emotion and 10 is the most intense and extreme. This will again help you put your feelings into perspective, as you'll realize that what you thought were overwhelming emotions aren't really that bad.

3. **Talk about what you feel**: Lastly, talk about your feelings with someone you trust. This can be a friend, your parents, siblings, teachers, or anyone you feel comfortable with. Talking about your everyday emotions will give you some practice in discussing feelings, which will make it a lot easier when you eventually need to talk about big and important emotions that affect you more deeply. If you don't want to talk about your feelings or don't feel like you have anyone you can trust enough, write about your emotions in your journal.

If you don't experience strong emotions, make a habit of doing these three steps three times a day. Even when you're not aware of experiencing any emotions, you will feel something, even if it's just feeling content. By doing this exercise frequently, you'll increase your awareness not just of the big and overpowering emotions but also of the little ones you feel daily.

Always remember that there are no good or bad emotions. The negativity that typically surrounds unhelpful emotions is created due to the behavior that is often associated with that feeling. Remember not to judge yourself for having these emotions. Instead, consider the impact that your thoughts may have on these feelings and whether these thoughts are fair and based on reality or not. In the next chapter, we'll discuss the connection that exists between your thoughts and emotions and how you can overcome the influence that your negative thoughts and limiting beliefs can have on your emotions.

3

CONNECTING YOUR THOUGHTS TO YOUR FEELINGS AND BEHAVIORS

None of us are immune to the various challenges that life brings. We all go through tough times where we don't see a way out or know how we'll overcome our difficulties. And, while our struggles are uniquely ours, there is one challenge that affects everyone: We all need to make sure that we maintain a healthy connection between our thoughts, feelings, and behaviors, and the situations that we create for ourselves.

Understanding this connection is an integral part of behavioral therapy. Once you're able to successfully manage this, you'll set yourself up to create the life and future you want.

UNDERSTANDING THOUGHTS, FEELINGS, AND BEHAVIORS

Before we go into detail about how this connection works, let's make sure you understand the three terms. We've already discussed emotions, but do you know what the term "thoughts" entails?

Your thoughts go beyond simply what you're thinking at a specific moment. They include your perceptions of everything in your life and determine the attitude you'll adopt when facing difficulties. Your thoughts are influenced by everything you know about life, including your past experiences and fears about the future. Without realizing it, these may result in baseless negative thoughts or limiting beliefs that keep you from living your best life.

Then, we have the term "behaviors." These are the actions that we take, which can be deemed appropriate or inappropriate, or simply good or bad. Every time we decide to behave in a specific way, this decision is influenced by the thoughts and emotions we're experiencing at that moment.

This is where this important connection comes into play and can result in a vicious cycle that can be difficult to break free from our thoughts and determine our emotions. Our emotions dictate our behavior. Our behavior creates situations. And the situations we find ourselves in sway our thoughts and can easily lead to us developing even more unhelpful thoughts and limiting beliefs.

Let's look at an example of this. You may have struggled with mathematics in the past and have since developed negative thoughts whenever you step into math class or have to do math homework. This has led you to create the limiting belief that you're not good at math. As a result, you're overcome by unhelpful emotions whenever you just hear the word "math." These feelings include frustration, anger, and even hatred for the subject. Because of these intense feelings, you stop trying your best: You don't concentrate in math class, and you don't try to understand the various math problems you have to solve. This has resulted in your math marks dropping even more, causing even more unhelpful and limiting thoughts, such as believing that you're too dumb to understand math and will never be able to do this.

Since we are all creatures of habit, breaking this cycle can be difficult, especially when the same cycle has repeated itself more than once. But if you change your negative thoughts about math the first time you started to struggle with the subject, from believing that you're not good at math to understanding that you may need to ask for help with this subject, you could've avoided all the resulting negativity in your life. You might even have realized that you only had challenges with a single aspect of math, not the subject as a whole.

THE ABC MODEL

There are many ways in which you can start to break the cycle of your thoughts, emotions, and behaviors. An effective method to accomplish this is by practicing the ABC model. It's built on the premise that you don't have to change your environment to feel better but rather transform any irrational beliefs you may have into rational ones by acknowledging and accepting the emotions you may experience and then choosing how you want to respond. In this case, the ABC doesn't represent the alphabet; the A stands for antecedents of activating events, the B for beliefs, and the C for consequences:

- **Antecedents of activating events**: This is the event that prompts your unhelpful thoughts and intense emotions. It can be a major event, such as being dumped by your crush or a loved one dying, or something minor, such as someone ignoring or speaking rudely to you. Anything that prompts you to have strong

thoughts and emotions can be considered an antecedent.
- **Beliefs**: This is where the work of the ABC model is done, as this directly influences your emotions and behaviors or the outcome of the event. These beliefs can be divided into two categories:
- **Irrational beliefs**: These are the rigid, illogical, and sometimes extreme beliefs that can consume you. When you're captured by these beliefs, you believe that more negative things will follow. If you continue to hold onto these beliefs, you may find yourself in a deep, dark pit of high levels of anxiety and depression. An example of this would be how you react if someone is rude to you. You may start to believe that this is because that person hates you or that you're an extremely unlikable person.
- **Rational beliefs**: These are the logical beliefs that are flexible, logical, and built on your preferences. They allow you to have a high level of acceptance, not just for others but also for yourself, and let you see the bigger picture in whatever you do or happens to you. Let's go back to the same example above of someone being rude to you. If you have rational beliefs,

you'll seek other possible explanations, such as the person's rudeness being a result of them having a difficult day or that they were simply preoccupied and didn't mean to be rude.

As we've discussed, all your beliefs will result in emotions. These may not always be what's considered positive emotions but always remember that even the most unhelpful emotions can have positive consequences. The goal of the ABC model isn't to avoid these emotions but rather to change the way you view your beliefs (or thoughts) and your emotions accordingly.

- **Consequences**: This is how you respond to the activating event according to the beliefs that you've allowed yourself to have. This is where the impact of the ABC model is felt. If you've allowed yourself to have irrational beliefs, your response may be over-the-top, leading to you potentially regretting your behavior. But, if you're acting on rational beliefs, you'll be able to respond in a calm manner where you can allow your unhelpful emotions to have a positive effect on your life. Continuing with the example from above, if you've allowed irrational beliefs to control your consequences, you may feel so bad about yourself that you believe that you'll never be liked by anyone again. Alternatively, if you follow your rational beliefs, you'll realize that the best thing you can do is wait for the other person to calm down before you decide whether you want to talk to them about something that upsets them.

Many people prefer to extend the ABC model to the ABCDE model. Here, the D stands for disputation of beliefs, and the E for new effects or energization. This is where you decide whether your beliefs have any validity and then focus on how your changed behavior can improve your life and relationships with others.

Now that you have a better understanding of the ABC model, implementing it in your life may feel overwhelming. To help make this easier, you can follow these three easy steps:

1. Track your self-talk: The first step is to come to terms with your inner dialogue, as this will help you understand your thoughts and feelings, especially when you're in a difficult situation. Ask yourself questions such as: What exactly happened? What are you thinking? What are you feeling? What are you telling yourself? What are your values? What are you thinking about the other people involved in the situation? For each situation, consider your ABCs and make notes of:

- What was the activating event that led to your thoughts and emotions?
- What are your beliefs regarding this situation? How are you feeling?
- How do you typically react to these events? What are the consequences of your reactions?

2. Consider your results: Once you've written down everything you can about your ABCs, read over your notes to consider your results. Look specifically for any patterns in your thinking, especially the specific consequences that your beliefs—both your irrational and rational ones—have on your life. If you find that you have irrational beliefs that you need to work on, you can continue to the third step.

3. Use disputation and energization: When you dispute your unhelpful beliefs or thoughts, you carefully consider the assumptions that you may have made. Are your thoughts valid? What evidence do you have that your thoughts or beliefs are true? Once you know whether you need to change your beliefs, you can go over to energization, where you consider the new effects that your changed beliefs may have on your life. Let's look at another example of how you can put it all together. To make this even more clear, we'll use an example where you have an irrational belief:

4. Activating event: You have to work in a team on a big school project. One of your teammates openly criticizes your idea.

5. Irrational belief: My teammate is right. I never have good ideas. I've also just embarrassed myself by telling my dumb idea to everyone. I'm such a loser.

6. Consequences: I feel horrible about myself and have lost my confidence. In the future, I will keep quiet and not share my ideas. I will just do as I'm told.

7. Disputation: In thinking about what happened and my beliefs about the event, I realize that I may have overreacted. I've had many good ideas in the past and will have more in the future.

8. Energization: In the future, I will make sure I think about my ideas in more detail so that I can explain them better to others. My next idea will be successful. I won't allow others to break my confidence again.

It can be difficult to change your negative thoughts or beliefs, especially when you've been struggling with these unhelpful convictions for a while. To help you with this, we'll next discuss how you can go about challenging your negative thoughts and beliefs.

CHALLENGING NEGATIVE THOUGHTS

We've already looked at how unhelpful thoughts and beliefs can influence your emotions and the outcomes of events, but it goes further than that. These thoughts and beliefs can also severely affect your mental health and lead to extremely low self-esteem, stress, anxiety, and depression. Once you're able to free yourself from your negative thoughts and beliefs, you can learn to cope with negative feedback and criticism, practice acceptance, and replace your negativity with more positive vibes.

While therapy can help you deal with these thoughts and beliefs, there are many different techniques you can use at home to help you evaluate your thoughts so that you can identify the negativity that's bringing you down and then replace it with helpful thoughts and beliefs that will help you thrive in life.

The first step is to practice mindfulness to increase your self-awareness so that you can identify your negative thoughts. By being present in the moment, you increase your awareness of the impact that your thoughts and beliefs have on your emotions and reactions. Now, instead of just being aware of them, ask yourself if your thoughts or beliefs are helping you move forward in life. What purpose is this thought or belief serving in your life?

Once you've identified your unhelpful thoughts or beliefs, be on the lookout for any patterns in your thinking. Some of the most common ones include:

- **Black-and-white thinking**: If you believe things are either one way or another, then you may be engaging in black-and-white thinking. For example, you believe that you are either wrong or right, or good or bad.
- **Jumping to conclusions**: This is when you constantly make negative assumptions, regardless of whether there is any evidence to show that you may be wrong.
- **Catastrophizing**: You always believe that the worst will happen without even considering reality or potential positive possibilities.
- **Overgeneralization**: When you've had one bad experience, you believe that all similar events in the future will be just as negative.
- **Labeling**: If you constantly label yourself in a negative way, you'll start to believe that these labels are the truth, whether there's any evidence to back them up or not.
- **"Should" statements**: This creates a negative connotation for anything you may say or think.

It gives the impression that you have to do things instead of wanting to do them. For example, if you say that you "should" work on your project, you'll immediately feel negative about it. But, if you change this to say that you want to complete your project so that you can have more free time later, you'll feel more positive about your task.
- **Emotional reasoning**: This happens when you believe something is true simply because you have a specific emotional response to it. For example, you believe that if you feel nervous about something, you'll fail at doing it, or if you feel scared, your life may be in danger.
- **Personalization and blame**: If you always take things personally or blame yourself for things that aren't necessarily your fault or within your control, you may engage in personalization.

These negative thinking patterns can lead to high levels of anxiety, which can put a bad twist on even the most positive situations. However, once you've identified your unhelpful thoughts, you can work at replacing them with positive or helpful beliefs.

This process is referred to as cognitive restructuring and can be done by following these easy steps:

1. Ask yourself whether your thoughts are realistic. In what way is this realistic? How sure are you that your imagination, assumptions, or limiting beliefs haven't affected your thoughts?
2. Think about similar experiences you may have had in the past. Are your thoughts now similar to what happened then?
3. Do you think your memories of this past event may influence your current thoughts? Is this influence helpful in any way? Will it bring you closer to a positive outcome?
4. Are there any alternative possibilities that I haven't considered yet? What are these? Why am I not thinking about them?
5. What can you gain by continuing with these thoughts? What do you stand to lose? Is there any good that can come from continuing with these thoughts?
6. Is there a pattern to your thinking? Does it fall into one of the categories listed above?
7. How can you change your thoughts? What would you say to your best friend if they were struggling with the same problem? What advice would you give them?

8. What can you do to convince yourself to follow this same advice?
9. What positive or helpful thoughts can I replace my negative thoughts with?

When it comes to replacing your thoughts with helpful ones, make sure you keep this realistic so that you don't overpromise yourself with over-the-top positive ones. These types of thoughts will set you up for future negative beliefs and won't be helpful in the long run. For example, if you feel like a failure after not making the sports team, you shouldn't replace these thoughts with ones of becoming the first-choice player for the team. Instead, be realistic and change your thought to something like, "I'm going to practice hard to try to make the team in the future," or "I'm going to try my best, and if I don't make the team, it will be okay." This type of thinking will also help fill your mind with the self-compassion you'll need should things not go your way.

Managing your negative thoughts and subsequent emotions and behaviors more effectively will be extremely helpful when you're going through times of high stress. In the next chapter, we'll look at distress tolerance and discuss more techniques you can implement into your daily life.

4

DISTRESS TOLERANCE SKILLS

Stress is part of our daily lives. No matter how much you try to avoid it, there will always be things that happen in your life or incidents of stress that may throw your life into disarray. These can be physical stress—where your life may be in danger—or emotional stress. If you can't manage these difficult times effectively, it can have far-reaching effects and impact your mental health as well.

Learning to deal with your physical and emotional stress without feeling overwhelmed falls under distress tolerance, one of the four pillars of DBT. These skills are often referred to as crisis survival skills, as they will help you overcome any stressful situations, whether real or perceived. You can even use these skills to help you cope with intense emotions, especially when you experience a few conflicting emotions at the same time.

When you go through times of intense distress, you may struggle to cope, which may lead you to behave in a destructive manner. This behavior, which in severe cases can include self-harming or abusing alcohol and other substances, can help distract you from the difficult moment and emotions you're experiencing. It can also mean avoiding the situation altogether, which may result in even more emotional pain as, eventually, your troubles will find their way to you. Crisis survival skills are short-term strategies that will help you cope with the emotional stress and pain you experience and will help you avoid behaving in these destructive manners.

LEARNING TO SELF-SOOTHE

When you're experiencing moments of high stress, your body's limbic system, often called the fight-or-flight, or freeze response, activates. While you're in this state, your body releases more stress hormones, such as cortisol and adrenaline, to help you make the necessary decisions to keep you safe from the perceived stress you may experience. These increases in hormone levels can make it difficult for you to practice the necessary coping techniques. This is why self-soothing can be so valuable.

Self-soothing basically refers to what you do to calm yourself down. Many people can self-soothe naturally—think of babies sucking their thumbs or toddlers holding onto their favorite soft toy or blanket during times of distress. As you grow older, these methods will change, and if you're not careful, you may resort to negative habitual behaviors, such as smoking.

Think about what you do when you're experiencing high levels of stress. Do you have any self-soothing methods that calm you down in times of distress? And if so, how effective are they? If you don't have any of these calming behaviors yet, don't feel alone; many people never develop their own self-soothing techniques.

Luckily, there are many self-soothing techniques you can teach yourself. One of these is using your five senses to bring you back to and ground you in the present moment. You can do this by:

- **See**: Look at everything around you. What colors and textures do you see?
- **Hear**: What can you hear? If there are no distinct sounds in your environment, focus on the sound of your breathing.

- **Touch**: What can you feel? Touch the chair you're sitting on, the material of your clothes, or even your own hair or skin.
- **Taste**: What can you taste? If you have something to drink or snack on close by, pay close attention to how this feels in your mouth.
- **Smell**: Lastly, inhale deeply through your nose and take in all the smells. If there are no strong smells or if you can't smell due to a blocked nose, look at things in your environment that typically have a strong scent and visualize yourself smelling them.

You can also use the same technique by honing in on your five senses with a specific object that you can hold, such as a piece of popcorn or a grape. Look at the textures and colors; feel the texture; smell it; taste it; and listen to how it sounds in your mouth as you chew on it.

LOOK AT THE PROS AND CONS

When we are in crisis mode, we tend to make decisions based on our emotions. While these decisions may feel right at the time, they may have long-term consequences that we didn't consider before we made them.

You may regret these rash and impulsive decisions, often when it's too late to turn back.

If you're struggling with deciding how you should handle a distressing situation, consider making a quick pros and cons list. Take a sheet of paper, fold it in half, and jot down all the reasons you should make a positive decision on the left side and all the negatives on the right side. This will not only help you to think about your options in a logical manner where you consider all the different aspects of your decision but also give you a few minutes to pause so that you can make your decision in a calm manner.

STOP TECHNIQUE

Another method you can use to bring more calmness to your life is the STOP technique. This technique, built on the acronym that stands for stop, take a breath, observe, and proceed, will only take a minute or even less to do. And, since the name of the technique literally tells you to stop, it's very easy to do.

Let's look at the four steps you can follow:

Stop what you are doing: Take a moment to pause whatever you're doing. Since this exercise can be done quickly, you can even do it in the middle of an exam when you're struggling with a difficult question or when you're dealing with confusing thoughts. Remember, the purpose of this isn't to fight your thoughts or clear your mind but to mentally make the decision to break your attention from what you're doing and give yourself a minute to distract yourself from the stress you're facing.

Take a breath: Focus on your breathing as you would while you're meditating. Inhale deeply through your nose and exhale through your mouth. Let your breathing settle into a deep rhythm so that you can ground yourself in the present moment.

Observe: This is arguably one of the most important aspects of this exercise, as it gives you the opportunity to check in with yourself. You should not only observe your external environment but also your internal sensations:

- What is going on around you? What is in your immediate environment? What is in your external environment that upsets you? What external factors can you block out?
- How does your body feel? Are you experiencing any pain? Does any part of your body feel tense? Use your senses to do a quick check on what you're seeing, hearing, smelling, touching, and tasting.

- What emotions are you feeling? How intense are these emotions?
- What thoughts are you having? What evidence do you have to prove the validity of your thoughts? Are your thoughts based on assumptions or judgments?

Proceed: Once you're done with your observations, you can proceed with your tasks. Use what you've just discovered from this exercise to help you cope with your challenges. For example, if you're in the middle of an exam, your quick STOP technique will help you to limit the overwhelm you're feeling, which may either be enough to answer that question or make the decision to skip over that one for now and answer the rest of the paper. Or, if you're in a difficult conversation, this technique may help you realize that you're too tired or overwhelmed to have a meaningful conversation and may have to request that this conversation be continued on another day.

RADICAL ACCEPTANCE

There may be times when nothing you do will make any difference to your situation or how you're feeling. In these times, radical acceptance will help you embrace your reality without any judgment.

This technique can be difficult to implement at first, as you will have to make peace with your reality without trying to change it. This can result in a lot of anxiety for some people. However, once you're able to accept that some situations aren't within your control and act only on the things that you do have control over, you can find the peace you need to overcome the distress that these situations may cause, as you will no longer feel any pressure to fix them.

When you're in a difficult situation, take a few minutes to observe the problem by practicing the STOP technique. Then, ask yourself what you can do to change the situation. If you can't come up with real actions you can take to improve the situation, accept that you have no control over it. Since you'll realize that it's not your responsibility to solve the problems or change the situation, you can free yourself from whatever is happening and focus your attention on your next step to get yourself out of the situation.

These techniques will not only help you deal with stressful situations but will also help you regulate your emotions more effectively. In the next chapter, we'll look at different techniques that were specifically designed to help with managing emotions more effectively.

5

EMOTIONAL REGULATION SKILLS

Emotional regulation, or managing your emotions effectively, is another pillar of DBT and, as we've discussed, goes hand-in-hand with controlling your negative thoughts and limiting beliefs to improve your behavior. While we've already discussed emotions in some detail, let's now look at another aspect of emotions: primary and secondary emotions.

Your primary emotion is the first emotion. When you're feeling happy, your primary emotion will be happiness, and when you're feeling sad, your primary emotion will be sadness. But, when you're feeling ashamed over how angry you got, anger will be your primary emotion, while shame will be your secondary one.

While it's important to consider both emotions when it comes to emotional regulation, your main focus should be on your primary emotion, as the secondary emotion comes simply as a result of the first one. This is a mistake that many people make, as they'll feel so overwhelmed by the secondary emotion that they forget to look at the root of the problem, or the first emotion. For example, the shame you feel after having an angry outburst can be so overpowering that you focus only on how embarrassed you are and how bad you're feeling for overreacting and forget to work on the reasons why you were angry in the first place.

There are, however, times when your secondary emotion will be the same as your primary one. For example, you may feel angry over being angry, such as when you're angry with your sibling for wearing your clothes, or you may feel angry with yourself over being angry about something so minimal. Or, you may feel sad about not being allowed to go out with your friends and then feel sad that this makes you feel so sad. In these cases, make sure that your secondary emotion is, in fact, the same as your primary one, and then work on dealing with the cause of your primary one.

There are also a few myths about emotions that many people choose to believe but should be debunked sooner rather than later, as they will keep you in a state of emotional dysregulation. One of these myths is that feeling emotions makes you weak. This is so far removed from the truth. Emotions are natural, and everyone gets emotional from time to time. The weakness that is often associated with emotions is a result of how you misbehave as a result of your thoughts and feelings.

Another common myth is that it's only okay to have positive emotions. As we've discussed, there is no such thing as positive and negative emotions. The negativity that's often associated with these emotions is, again, a result of how you react to your feelings.

The last myth that we'll discuss is that it's not okay to show others when you're emotional. This implies that you need to keep your emotions hidden from the people around you, which often causes people to avoid their emotions. This results in people not dealing with their emotions, which only serves to give this specific emotion more power in their lives. When you allow yourself to feel an emotion and then decide how you want to behave, you take the power away from the emotion while still acknowledging its existence and the reason for feeling it.

Always keep these in mind as you work on your emotions and build your own personalized emotional regulation toolkit.

BUILDING YOUR EMOTION REGULATION TOOLKIT

Just like every person's emotions will be different, their toolkit for managing these feelings will also differ. In this book, we discuss various CBT and DBT techniques that are excellent at helping you control how you feel and respond to your feelings. Even exercises that help you cope with other aspects, such as distress tolerance and challenging your negative thoughts, will also help you better manage your feelings.

I encourage you to try all of these strategies out and make notes of the ones you find to help you calm your racing thoughts and emotions. Some will work for you, while others may be less effective; this can be a process of trial and error. But finding strategies that work for you is how you'll go about creating an emotion regulation toolkit that's tailor-made for you.

Also, remember the three golden rules of emotional regulation:

1. If you want to experience more of a specific emotion, focus on behaving in ways that bring forth those emotions.
2. If you want to reduce an emotion, pinpoint the thoughts or events that bring these unhelpful

emotions to the forefront and what you can do to eliminate them from your life.
3. If you want to gain control over your emotions, you need to believe that you can overcome any challenges you may face and choose to regain power over your feelings and subsequent actions.

OPPOSITE ACTION

Many times, we act on our emotions without giving them any thought. When you're sad, you'll want to cry; when you're happy, you'll want to smile; and when you're angry, you'll want to scream. When you practice Opposite Action in your life, you'll choose to respond differently to how you were biologically wired.

Let's look at a few common emotions you'll likely experience and how you can choose an opposite action to manage these feelings:

- Anger makes us want to scream, attack, or defend ourselves. An opposite action shows kindness, such as walking away from an aggravating event.
- Shame makes us want to isolate ourselves. An opposite action will let us keep our chins up,

make eye contact with others, and stand up for ourselves.
- Fear makes us want to hide or escape the perceived danger we're facing. An opposite action will imply that we build courage and stay involved in the fearful situation.
- Depression is another emotion that makes us want to distance ourselves from others. An opposite action will require us to actively seek out happiness and positivity in our lives.
- Disgust makes us want to reject or avoid others or the aggravating situation. An opposite action will help us find the inner peace to push through any disgust we may experience.
- Guilt makes us want to feel bad about ourselves and our actions. An opposite action encourages us to resist any bad feelings and apologize for anything we might have done wrong.

Always keep in mind that there are certain emotional responses that you should never ignore, as these are vital for your own survival. Examples of this include:

- **Thirst**: When you're feeling thirsty, you should have a sip of water to stay hydrated.

- **Hunger**: When you're hungry, you should have something to eat, as you need food to fuel your body.
- **Fatigue**: When you're tired, see this as your body telling you that you need to rest.

At first, you may find it difficult to act contrary to what your biological instincts tell you to do. In these cases, it may be helpful to change your body position or even your environment completely. For example, if you're sitting while you're experiencing an intense emotion, stand up and walk around. Or, if you're inside, go outside.

COPING AHEAD

As you become more aware of your emotions and how you respond to certain situations, you can use the Coping Ahead technique to help you deal with your challenges more effectively. This exercise is all about preparing for difficult situations that may lie ahead, visualizing the challenging emotions you may experience, and planning how you want to respond to your difficulties. This will also help you reduce the stress you may experience.

While there are many ways of doing this, you can follow these basic steps to skillfully prepare to cope with emotional situations:

1. Describe the situation that may lead to intense or uncomfortable emotions. Visualize yourself in that situation so that you're fully aware of all the feelings that might start bubbling over. Be specific about the situation and name all these emotions that may keep you from performing at your best.
2. Next, decide how you'd like to cope with the situation or solve the problems you may face. Add as much detail as you possibly can, particularly how you'll keep yourself from giving in to your emotional urges.
3. Rehearse the situation and coping mechanisms until you feel comfortable, not just with the situation that might lie ahead but also with the emotions that may accompany it. Practice your actions, thoughts, emotions, and the different ways in which you might respond. Decide what you believe your best response will be by contemplating all the potential consequences you may face.
4. Now, think about overcoming the challenge you're facing and how you'll feel once you've

successfully managed your emotions and behaved in a more helpful manner.
5. End the exercise by practicing a few relaxation techniques so that you feel calm about what you're about to face and how you plan to overcome your challenge. In Chapter 7, we'll discuss a few relaxation techniques that will help you remain calm, regardless of how stressful your situation may seem.

Let's look at an example of this. If you hate talking in front of others and have to do a presentation as part of your school project, you may be overcome by fear and anxiety just at the thought of standing up to talk in front of your peers and teacher. To overcome this fear, you can plan every aspect of your presentation and research your topic online to make sure you can answer any potential questions you may be asked. Artificial intelligence can also help you come up with some possible questions you may not have thought about. Then, once you feel confident in your knowledge, practice delivering your speech over and over, first to yourself in the mirror, then by recording yourself and listening to it again, and then in front of your family. Add some deep breathing exercises to this routine, as this may also help you to calm yourself down.

CHECKING THE FACTS

In many cases, the actual situation that we find ourselves in isn't the cause of our emotional difficulties but rather our own interpretation of the situation. This is typically caused by our unhelpful thoughts and limiting beliefs, which, as we've discussed, are the results of our pasts and our perceptions of things, ourselves, and other people. This can warp our minds so much that we're unable to think clearly.

For example, you were expecting your crush to send you a message, but it's been hours since you last heard from them. While you sit staring at your phone, your mind immediately starts to race until you start finding the problems within yourself and blaming yourself for being unlikeable. Eventually, you're so deeply distressed that you make yourself believe that no one will ever like you or message you again. You don't even consider the possibility that they may simply be so busy with something else that they don't have time to talk to others or that your phone might be on silent, resulting in you missing a message.

To help you deal with these types of difficult emotions, you can do a quick fact-check to make sure your emotions are valid and determine which emotions you'd like to change. These questions can help you with this:

- What feeling do you want to change? Why do you want to change this emotion?
- What was the event that led to you feeling this emotion? Consider if you have any negative thoughts, limiting beliefs, or cognitive distortions that may cause these emotions.
- What assumptions do you have about this event? Are there other interpretations that you might not have considered? Place yourself in someone else's shoes and consider how they would view it.
- Is there a real threat? Or are you assuming a non-existent threat? What is the possibility of this threat actually playing out? What other outcomes might there be?
- What will happen if this threat pans out? What consequences will I face? How will I be able to cope with this threat? Use the Coping Ahead technique to plan how you'll deal with this situation.
- Does your emotion fit the facts? Are you overreacting to your problems?

RIDE THE WAVE

If you often experience intense emotions, this exercise can help you overcome the challenges you may face. In this exercise, you'll visualize your emotions as waves in the ocean. Think of how a wave breaks on the shore, pushes over the sand, and recedes back into the ocean. While it breaks, it may seem violent and overpowering, but the longer you let it flow naturally over the sand, it becomes less and less potent until it eventually loses all its momentum and naturally dies down. Nothing you can do to the wave can change this natural process.

Emotions are exactly like waves. When something happens that evokes an intense reaction, it's like a wave breaking. Just as a wave can move anything in its path, your emotions can do exactly the same. But, in the same way that the wave will lose its momentum until it eventually dies down, your emotion will decrease in intensity until it eventually retracts back into the "ocean" or your mind.

When you're riding the emotional wave, you allow yourself to mentally experience your emotion without reacting to it. Visualize the wave while you do this, as this will remind you that just like the wave will lose its momentum, your emotion will do the same, whether you react to it or not. Remind yourself that just like you can't change the waves crashing on the shore, you can't always do anything to change your emotions. But, if you give it enough time, the intensity of your emotion will naturally decrease until it either becomes more manageable or goes away by itself.

FIND ENJOYMENT IN LIFE

Actively seeking joy in life can be a very helpful tool for countering challenging feelings. This can be seen as another way to self-soothe, which we discussed in the previous chapter, where you'll use your senses to ground yourself in your present reality. In this exercise, you'll choose to do things that make you feel better and calm your mind.

Below, I've listed some activities that you may consider doing, but I encourage you to create your own list of enjoyable pastimes. In the past, these would've simply been things you enjoyed doing, but now they will become self-soothing activities to help you cope with your strong emotions. Try to incorporate as many of your senses as you can into these activities, and if you can become more physically active while doing it, that's even more of a bonus.

Enjoyment Activity Suggestions		
Have a warm bath.	Recycle old things.	Watch a movie.
Read your favorite book.	Find something to laugh about.	Think about a pleasant memory.
Sit outside in the sun.	Listen to music.	Go for a jog.
Spend 30 minutes doing a hobby.	Go out with your friends.	Eat your favorite meal.
Learn a new skill.	Practice a new sport.	Spend time in nature.
Sing and dance around the house.	Go to the beach and look for shells.	Repeat positive affirmations.
Do something artistic.	Do something spontaneously.	Learn a new musical instrument.
Make a gift for someone.	Help out with cooking.	Create your own garden.
Daydream about your future.	Binge on your favorite series on TV.	Volunteer at a community organization.
Spend time with animals.	Journal your thoughts and emotions.	Have a picnic in the park.
Ground yourself with meditation.	Build a puzzle.	Talk to your best friend.
Think about your good qualities.	Watch the sunrise or sunset.	Decorate your room.
Take a nap.	People watch in the park.	Plan your future.

The better you're able to manage your emotions, the more your communication with others will improve. This will help you build good relationships with others. In the next chapter, we'll look at various techniques you can implement to improve your interpersonal effectiveness.

6

INTERPERSONAL EFFECTIVENESS SKILLS

As you grow older, your relationships will change. As a young child, your parents or caregivers are the most important people in your life, and you'll not only want to spend as much time with them as possible but also do whatever you can to make them happy. But this changes when you get older. When you're a teenager, this changes. Suddenly, you'll prefer to spend time with your friends over your parents, and peer pressure may make you do many things that you'll one day regret.

Apart from this, your many strong emotions may make it difficult to communicate with others. You may feel like other people (especially your parents) don't understand you or the slang language you might use, or you may get so short-tempered that you explode over things that they don't see as a big issue. All of this can severely impact your relationships with others.

Unfortunately, there is no prescription or one-size-fits-all approach that will fix the relational problems you may have. But, since interpersonal effectiveness forms one of the pillars of DBT, there are many different techniques you can implement in your life that can make this process easier, starting with improving your communication skills.

EFFECTIVE COMMUNICATION

How you communicate with others forms the foundation on which all your connections with others are built. If you can effectively communicate with others, you can not only tell them how you feel and what you want and don't want, but you'll also be able to prove to others how much you've grown as a person. This may help you gain more independence, something you'll desperately want as you mature into adulthood.

While you may communicate differently with your parents, teachers, or friends, the basics of communication remain the same: active listening, respecting others, and dealing with conflict and other negative situations.

Listen More and Talk Less

Let's start with active listening, which is arguably the biggest problem many people have in their communication with others. Too many of us are guilty of not listening when someone talks to us. We might hear what they're saying but start to think about how we want to answer them before the other person is done talking. This results in us listening to respond instead of listening to truly understand what they're saying.

There is a reason why we all have two ears but only one mouth. We need to spend twice as much time listening as talking. When you show others that you're trying to understand what they're saying, they'll likely be more willing to share more with you, increasing your connection with them.

Let's look at some tips that can help you improve your communication:

- Stop whatever you're busy with when someone talks to you. Look into their eyes, and don't interrupt them while they're talking. Let them finish, and then take a few breaths before you answer. This will also help you calm yourself down before you respond.
- Make sure your body language shows that you're calm. Try your best not to roll your eyes,

sigh, or cross your arms or legs. Also, consider your facial expressions, as your face may say much more than you want.

- Understand that others may have different opinions than yours. Just because you may not agree with what they're thinking doesn't mean that they are wrong. They simply see things from their point of view. You may even learn from their way of thinking.
- Use "I" statements instead of "you" statements. When you do this, you'll immediately focus your attention on how you're feeling instead of accusing them of anything. For example, you can say, "I don't like it when my calls are ignored," which will be accepted more positively than saying, "You always ignore me," or you can say, "I would like to have more independence," which is more positive than saying, "You don't want me to grow up; you treat me like a little child."
- Never use sarcasm when talking to others. Also, avoid criticizing them. Focus only on the facts, and tell them directly what you want or need.
- Never assume you know what the other person is thinking. You're not a mind-reader. The only way you will know what others are thinking or feeling is by listening to what they're saying.

Show Your Respect

Mutual respect is extremely important in any relationship, as it shows the other person that you care about them and value them enough to treat them the way you want to be treated. Respect is a two-way street, and regardless of what you might want to believe, it has to be earned. The easiest way to do this is by treating the other person with the same respect you expect from them.

While the communication tips we've discussed above will already go a long way toward showing the other person respect, the following can help build a strong connection with them:

- Make an effort to spend quality time with them by doing things that they enjoy, not just what you want to do. Show them that you care about them and want to learn about their interests.
- Give them space and privacy when necessary. If they tell you they don't have time or can't do something with you, you shouldn't read too much into this. Remember, they have their own lives and things they have to do; you can't expect them to leave whatever is going on in their lives to jump whenever you call.

- Show interest in their interests. Asking about their preferences doesn't mean you have to be interested in the same things. It simply shows that you're interested in the things that they enjoy and would like to learn more about them.
- Create a caring relationship with the other person by celebrating their achievements with them, forgiving their mistakes, helping them solve their problems, and supporting them when they're going through difficult times.
- Always make time to have fun and laugh together. Laughter will not only help you deal with difficult emotions; it will also help you bond. Always remember that good feelings build a good relationship.

Turn Negatives Into Positives

No matter how good your communication and interpersonal skills may be, you're bound to experience some level of conflict with other people. This is because everyone has different points of view and their own thoughts and emotions that they'll try to protect. But, with proper communication skills, you can limit the impact that this conflict will have on your relationships.

Conflict doesn't have to be a negative thing that can destroy relationships. If you're careful with how you manage your conflict, you can actually use it to your advantage to build even stronger connections with others:

- Pick your battles carefully. Every conflicting situation doesn't have to turn into a fight. Make a rule of only fighting with others over things that are really important to you or threaten your safety.
- Ask for a timeout if you're feeling overwhelmed by the conflict. You can simply tell the other person that you are upset and need a break from the conversation to calm yourself down and collect your thoughts.
- Look for solutions together. Instead of telling the person how the conflict must be resolved, explain what you'd like to achieve or can't tolerate in your life, and listen to their input as well. Aim at finding solutions that you're both happy with.
- If you have to criticize the other person, do this in a constructive manner by leaving the emotions to one side and stating only the facts. Also, never underestimate the impact that

compliments can have, so always acknowledge the good that they're doing.
- Always apologize when you're wrong. By making yourself vulnerable, you'll show the other person that you care about the relationship and are committed to them.

DEAR MAN TECHNIQUE

There may be times when talking nicely to others won't be enough to convince them of your ideas. In these times, it may be necessary to take a more assertive approach while being mindful of maintaining a healthy relationship with them. This is where the DEAR MAN technique can be so helpful. Let's look at the seven steps in this technique:

- **D—Describe the situation**: Always stick to the facts when discussing the situation. It can be helpful to remove yourself from the situation and describe it as if you weren't directly involved.
- **E—Express how you feel**: Now, use your "I" statements to tell the person how the situation has affected you and made you feel. Remember not to point fingers or place any blame on the other person.

- **A—Assert yourself**: Tell the other person directly what you want and need in a respectful and non-aggressive way. Remember, you're trying to maintain a healthy relationship while resolving the conflict, so do this in the nicest way you can.
- **R—Reinforce your request**: Tell the person how much it will mean to you if they're willing to do what you're asking of them. Alternatively, you can simply thank the person for being willing to have this discussion with you.
- **M—Mindfulness**: Stay present in the moment, avoid any distractions, and ignore attacks. Remember the reason why you started this discussion with the person, and stick to what you want and believe you deserve.
- **A—Appear confident**: Many people feel very uncomfortable when they have to be assertive and tell others what they want from them. No matter how unsure you may feel about yourself, try your best to appear confident by making eye contact and speaking in a calm and clear manner.
- **N—Negotiate**: The other person might not be willing to do what you expect them to do. Interpersonal effectiveness is also not about enforcing your will on others but rather

reaching an agreement that both parties are comfortable with. This may mean that you have to negotiate on certain points. Know what you're willing to negotiate on before you start the conversation, listen to what the other person is saying, and see where you can compromise.

SETTING BOUNDARIES

Boundaries are like imaginary lines that you draw to tell others what you're okay with and what you definitely don't want. As a teenager, you may find yourself in many difficult situations that will require you to have strict boundaries to protect yourself. These are especially important when it comes to friends and dating partners, as they may ask you to do things that you either don't want to do or aren't ready for yet, such as drinking or having sex. You can even set specific boundaries with your parents, such as asking them to respect your privacy.

Even though it's extremely important to set certain boundaries, it can be difficult, as you're essentially forcing yourself to have difficult or comfortable situations with others. When you set a boundary, you also need to explain to the other person what the consequences will be if they don't respect it. This can be nerve-wracking, as someone who lacks emotional maturity might not understand your needs and limitations.

Although you can set boundaries for virtually every aspect of your life, some typical areas where teenagers need boundaries include when

- a romantic partner pushes you to become sexually active.
- a friend expects you to share your homework.
- you don't want to be involved in gossiping.
- a friend is bossy.
- someone wants to borrow money from you.
- someone tries to force you to do something you don't want to do.
- an adult touches you inappropriately.
- anyone disrespects your privacy.

The boundaries you need to set in your life may look completely different from these examples. Think about the areas in your life where you would like to see some change or where you feel uncomfortable. These are typically the aspects of your life where you'll benefit from setting boundaries. Make a list of the potential boundaries that you want to set, and then decide which one you want to start with.

I would recommend that you start with only one so that you're not overwhelmed by the process. As much as you may want to start with the biggest or most important boundary, I suggest you start with one that will be relatively easy to implement, as this will give you the confidence to set more important ones.

When you're ready to set your boundaries, you can follow these steps:

Identify your feelings: Before you set the boundary, you should know how you're feeling when someone does what you're trying to stop by setting the limitation. This will help you determine how urgent this boundary is and how strict you should be in implementing it.

Practice key phrases: To make it easier to set boundaries, practice some basic phrases that will help you either buy some time or say no in a polite but stern way. These can include:

- "No thank you; that's not something I'm comfortable with."
- "No thank you; I don't want to do that."
- "Let me think about it, and I'll get back to you."
- "I'll ask my parents and get back to you."

Be clear: Explain your boundaries in a clear and straightforward manner to the other person so that you can be sure that they understand exactly what you want and don't want. You can add as much detail as you want but don't feel pressured into giving them any information you might not be comfortable with. Remember to use your "I" statements when you explain your boundary. Ask the other person if they understand what you're saying to them, and give them the opportunity to ask any questions they may have about your boundary.

Explain the consequences: It's important that you make it clear that you won't tolerate it if your boundaries aren't respected. Always tell the other person what will happen if they don't adhere to your boundaries and oversteps again.

Decide on your non-negotiables: As with any other discussion, you need to be prepared that the other person may not immediately agree with your boundaries. To prepare for this, decide beforehand what aspects of your boundary are non-negotiables and how far you're willing to negotiate to find a compromise. Never agree to anything you're not comfortable with.

While you're busy setting your boundaries, you also need to be mindful of any boundaries the other person might have and make sure you give them the same level of respect that you expect from them. If you're unsure of any boundaries they might have, this might be a good time to ask them about their boundaries. This will open the conversation, and your interest in their limits may also make them more willing to listen and adhere to your boundaries.

Your mind and your body are closely connected, and if one isn't performing at its best, the other will struggle as well. This is why taking care of your physical well-being is so important for creating the mental and emotional wellness you need to thrive. In the next chapter, we'll discuss this in more detail and look at different ways you can improve your physical health to benefit your mental and emotional health.

7

MIND-BODY CONNECTION

Every feeling that you have has a physical sensation in your body. When you're feeling nervous, you feel it in the gut or the butterflies in your stomach. When you're experiencing anxiety, your heart races, and you may sweat more than usual. When you're feeling sad, tears roll down your cheeks as you cry. When you're happy, your facial muscles move to smile.

Since all your feelings have specific bodily sensations that define them, it's easy to see the connection between your body, or your physical health, and your mind, or your mental and emotional health. When your physical health is weak, your mental and emotional wellness will follow. Similarly, your mental health will struggle, and your emotional and physical well-being will suffer.

TAKING CARE OF YOUR PHYSICAL WELL-BEING

Improving your physical health is all about making sure you eat a healthy diet, are physically active, and get enough sleep every night. The benefits of living a healthy lifestyle will help you not only today in improving your emotional health but also when you get older and physical health ailments become more concerning. Let's look at the three aspects of physical health you can start working on immediately.

Healthy Eating Habits

The younger you start with healthy eating habits, the easier it will be to make this part of your new lifestyle that will benefit you for the rest of your life. This is particularly important if you have any body image difficulties that may result in you developing an eating disorder.

While it's always advisable to seek the professional insights of a dietitian, you can start to introduce some healthy habits, such as:

- **Stay hydrated**: It's important that you drink at least eight glasses of water daily. Alternatively, you can also drink a glass or two of milk. Try to limit your consumption of coffee, sugary drinks, and energy drinks (more on this below). Also, be careful of the amount of fruit juice you consume, as this often contains a lot more sugar and other calories than you might have thought.
- **Take care of your bones**: As a teenager, you need to consume a lot of calcium and vitamin D daily to help develop healthy and strong bones. Fish and orange juice are rich in vitamin D, or you can simply spend some time in the sun daily for your skin to absorb vitamin D from the sun. The vitamin D in your body will help you absorb more calcium from the foods you eat. You can increase your calcium intake by drinking milk and eating cheese and yogurt.
- **Up your iron intake**: Iron helps to support growth and is especially important for teenage girls, who are often at risk of having low iron levels. Red meat and iron are very good sources of iron. If you don't eat meat, you can get your iron from leafy green vegetables, nuts, beans, and lentils.
- **Snacks**: While it's important that you eat three meals per day, you also need to snack in

between, particularly on days when you're very active. Make sure you eat healthy snacks, such as fruit, vegetables, or nuts. If you crave chocolate, opt for dark chocolate, and choose popcorn over potato crisps.
- **Avoid energy drinks**: Many teenagers drink dangerously high amounts of energy drinks every day, especially when they are taking part in sports. Try your best to avoid this because energy drinks generally contain high levels of sugar, which can lead to weight gain, and caffeine, which can cause irregular heartbeats and anxiety.

Exercise and Movement

Physical activity is very important for your emotional health, as your body releases dopamine and serotonin, otherwise known as feel-good hormones when you're moving. There are different levels of physical activity, which are generally classified as follows:

- **Light activities**: These include all activities where your body is moving, such as leisurely walking, playing a musical instrument, or doing art.

- **Moderate activities**: These will increase your heart rate slightly, such as brisk walking, cycling, swimming, and dancing.
- **Vigorous activities**: These include activities that will require you to push your limits, such as taking part in sports with a lot of running and climbing, as well as muscle-building activities such as push-ups, squats, and lunges.

It is recommended that teenagers get at least one hour of vigorous activity three times a week, with moderate to light activity on the other days. Their physical activities should include at least two hours of muscle strengthening per week (*Physical activity for older children and teenagers*, 2018).

If you take part in sports at school, you may already get enough physical activity for your age. If not, you can create your own schedule of physical activity. These questions can help you plan your physical activity:

- How much exercise do you currently do? How much more do you need per week?
- For how long can you be active in one go? What time of the day is best for you to exercise?
- Do you have the space at home to be more active? Or do you have access to exercise

facilities? These can include a gym, a pool, or even just a local park.
- Who are your "active" friends that may help you get into the habit of exercising?
- What type of exercise do you want to do? What will help me stick to my workout program?

It's important that you consider your current lifestyle and schedule when you plan your own workout program. Also, think about the amount of time you spend doing homework, and if this takes up too much of your time, think of ways you can incorporate physical activity in between. This can include taking five-minute breaks to do yoga stretches, running around, or working at a standing desk.

Improve Your Sleeping Habits

Your sleeping habits may have a big impact on your physical, mental, and emotional health. Even though you may believe that you can cope with going to bed later at night, your body still needs between 8–10 hours of sleep every night. If you struggle to fall asleep earlier at night, consider trying out these tips:

- Create a relaxing bedtime routine, which can include having a warm bath, meditating, and reading a relaxing book. Stick with this routine

for at least three weeks to get your body used to it.
- Try to avoid screens for at least an hour before you go to bed. These screens emit a blue light that slows down your body's release of melatonin, the hormone that helps you fall asleep.
- Keep your bedroom cool and dark at night.
- Make your bedtime 10 minutes earlier. Stick to this for about a week before you move your bedtime another 10 minutes earlier. Doing this gradually will help your body adjust to this change easily.
- Make sure you get your exercise in early enough during the day so that your dopamine and serotonin levels have time to go down before you want to fall asleep.

RELAXATION TECHNIQUES

When your physical body is experiencing high levels of stress, your emotional health will suffer as you struggle to relax and manage your thoughts and emotions. While adopting a healthier lifestyle will already help your body find a sense of calm more easily, relaxation techniques can also be life-changing.

Relaxation techniques can be done literally anywhere, even in the middle of a stressful exam, and are extremely easy to learn. Let's start by discussing some deep breathing exercises.

Practicing Deep Breathing

Deep breathing may sound complicated, but all it actually means is to take some time to focus only on your breathing. This is a quick but powerful tool to ground yourself in a calm state of mindfulness so that you can become more deliberate in your actions.

The amount of time you spend on these exercises will depend on your stress levels. Some people prefer to do deep breathing for at least 5–10 minutes at a time, while others prefer to only spend about two minutes at a time on this practice. Some have included these exercises in their schedules at set times, while others do them as and when they need to calm themselves down. Experiment with this before you decide how often and for how long you want to do deep breathing to get the outcome you desire.

There are many different deep breathing techniques you can follow. When you do a cycle of deep breathing, repeat the technique of your choice to create a pattern of deep breathing.

Here are some of the most popular ones:

Pursed-lip breathing: This exercise is very helpful when you're busy with physical activities, such as lifting or climbing stairs.

- Relax your shoulders and neck.
- Close your mouth while you inhale through your nose for two counts.
- Purse your lips as if you're whistling.
- Exhale through your lips for four counts.

Diaphragmatic breathing: This is often referred to as belly breathing and is very effective in reducing stress.

- Lie on your back and bend your knees slightly. If you want, you can place a pillow under your knees for support.
- Put your left hand on your chest and your right hand on your stomach, just below your rib cage.
- Inhale slowly through your nose and pay attention to how your stomach is pressing against your right hand. Keep your left hand as still as possible.
- Tighten your abdominal muscles as you exhale through pursed lips.

Alternate nostril breathing: This is another effective breathing technique but should only be done when your nose isn't congested.

- Sit in a comfortable position.
- Lift your right hand to your nose and use your fingers to completely close your right nostril. Inhale deeply through your left nostril.
- Release your right nostril and lift your left hand to close your left nostril with your fingers. Exhale completely through your right nostril.
- Keep this position to inhale again through your right nostril, after which you swap again to close your right nostril and exhale through your left one.

Once you've inhaled and exhaled through both nostrils, you've completed one cycle of alternate nostril breathing. Continue with this to form a pattern of deep breathing.

Box breathing: This is a very easy exercise that can be done anywhere to quickly bring calm to your body and mind.

- Sit in a comfortable position. If you can, close your eyes so that you reduce as much distraction as you can.

- Inhale deeply through your mouth for four counts.
- Hold your breath for four counts.
- Exhale completely through your mouth for four counts.
- Hold your breath for four counts.

Progressive Muscle Relaxation

This relaxation technique is focused on the various muscle groups and combines mindfulness with deep breathing to help you not only become more aware of your body's various muscles but also find calmness. While a complete muscle relaxation session will take a few minutes, you can adapt it to your needs and do a shortened version within a minute or two in any environment.

To do this exercise, make sure you're sitting somewhere where you are comfortable, ideally with your legs stretched out in front of you. Put your phone on silent and eliminate as many other distractions as you can, such as switching the TV off. If you want to play calming music, you can, as long as it doesn't influence your focus.

Start with a few deep breathing exercises until you reach a calming rhythm. Then, you can start at either your hands or feet and work your way either up or down your body, tensing each muscle group for between 15 and 20 seconds before you release it. Pay close attention to how each muscle group feels before, during, and after you tense the muscles. Take a break of about 20 seconds before you either repeat the same muscle group again or move on to the next muscle. If you ever experience any pain while doing this exercise, you need to stop immediately and move on to the next group of muscles.

Practice mindfulness while you do this by focusing only on your breathing and the sensations in your muscles. If your mind wanders, simply accept your thoughts without judgment and bring your attention back to your breathing and the tensing and relaxing of your muscles.

You can follow these steps as you focus on your various muscle groups:

- **Feet**: Curl your toes and release. Then, push with your ankles to your left and release. Repeat this process to the right.
- **Legs**: Work on your legs by tightening your half muscles, then your shins, then your thighs, and releasing.
- **Buttocks**: Clench the muscles in your bum by squeezing your cheeks together and releasing.

- **Back**: Bend forward as far as you can and release. Arch your back and release.
- **Hands**: Make tight fists and release. Stretch your fingers out as wide as you can and release.
- **Arms**: Flex your biceps and release. Then, bend your arms at your elbows as far as you can and release.
- **Shoulders**: Bring your shoulders toward your ears and release.
- **Neck**: Gently push your neck backward and release. Then, bring your head to your left before you release. Repeat this process to your right. Finish off by bringing your chin to your chest before you release.
- **Mouth**: Purse your lips and release. Then, press your tongue against the roof of your mouth and release.
- **Face**: Smile as widely as you can and release.
- **Eyes**: Open your eyes wide and release. Then, close your eyes tightly and release.
- **Forehead**: Furrow your eyebrows in a deep frown and release.

While you're working on your emotional regulation and your physical health to improve your emotional health, you may discover that you're struggling with very specific emotions. These are typically the emotions that can easily have unhelpful consequences, such as anger, anxiety, stress, sadness, and depression. In the next chapter, we'll discuss tips on how you can better cope with these feelings.

8

COPING WITH SPECIFIC EMOTIONS

Your parents are likely constantly reprimanding you for overreacting to certain events, having angry outbursts, and even misreading situations to see the presence of hostile emotions when they're not there. This will make you feel even more confused than ever before. And, unless you really make an effort to cope with your strong emotions more effectively, you'll just continue to struggle.

This is because of the development of the teenage brain. As we've discussed, the prefrontal cortex of the brain, where emotions are regulated, only matures around the age of 25. This means that teenagers must rely on other parts of their brains to handle these feelings. When you use the back part of your brain, which is specifically sensitive to threats and dangers, you may seek out hostile emotions in others and see threats that don't really exist. While this isn't your fault or within your control, you can't help reacting in this way.

Understanding that your developing brain may result in your overreacting is a good first step in trying to cope with these intense feelings. Next, we'll discuss the strong emotions you may struggle with in more detail, as well as specific ways in which you can cope with them.

MANAGING YOUR ANGER

How often do you struggle with anger and angry outbursts, slamming the doors and rolling your eyes while you storm away from your aggravating situation? I'm sure if you really think about your own life, you may be shocked at how often you respond to a situation with anger.

As difficult as controlling your anger can be, there are many ways in which you can manage it more effectively:

- **It's okay to be angry**: Remind yourself that anger is a natural emotion that you're allowed to feel. Getting angry with others or in certain situations doesn't make you a bad person; it means you're human. As we've already discussed, you should never try to ignore or avoid your intense feelings but rather discover the cause of your anger and find better ways of dealing with these emotions.

- **Reach out**: When you're overcome by anger, give yourself a few minutes to calm down, but try to reach out to someone you trust as soon as you can. This can be a friend, sibling, parent, teacher, or anyone who will understand and support you. Explain to them as best you can why you're feeling angry but try your best to do this in a calm, collected manner. If you perhaps don't understand your own anger, simply tell them what you're feeling. They may be able to give you advice on how to deal with your situation or perhaps simply provide a listening ear.
- **Show respect**: No matter how frustrated you may feel with your feelings and situation, make sure you show others the respect that they deserve. Lashing out at others won't help you resolve the anger you may feel. Think twice about what you want to say and how you plan to say it.
- **Check-in with yourself**: Be mindful of how you're feeling and what's really happening in

your life. Pay attention to your body language and the tone you use when you talk to others. Always be kind to yourself. You're only human and are dealing with a lot of changes that can make it very difficult to cope with your challenges.

- **Remember the good**: Always remember that, just like you've experienced many happy times in the past, you will overcome any anger you feel and find happiness again in the future. Hold onto these memories and look at photos or old videos of happy times. This can distract you from your anger and help you find positivity again.

Create a "Calm Down" Kit

If you're struggling to restrain yourself when you're angry, you might benefit from creating a toolkit to help you calm down. Take some time to think about what usually helps you cool off. Include as many sensory items as you can in this kit, such as pictures of happy times you can look at, your favorite scented hand lotion or cologne to smell, a few sweets that you can taste, a list of your favorite songs you can listen to, or materials or textures you can touch.

You can even create a virtual tool kit in a folder on your phone where you can store photos, videos, songs, or instructions for breathing exercises that can help you find calm.

DEALING WITH ANXIETY

Everyone experiences stress and anxiety from time to time, especially before and during a big event, such as an exam, or while you're waiting for important news, such as getting your exam results. Even young children get anxious at times. Think of their fears of the dark or having monsters under the bed. As you become a teenager, the source of your anxiety will become a lot different. Suddenly, you don't worry about monsters or insects anymore. Now, the biggest source of your worries is likely centered around yourself: your performance at school, your body, how others see you, and your negative thoughts and unhelpful emotions.

While some levels of anxiety and stress can actually be helpful in that they can help you make important decisions, they can also severely disrupt your life.

And, since high levels of anxiety can lead to many more serious mental health conditions if left untreated, it's important that you're aware of the most common symptoms of anxiety in teenagers:

- extreme and recurring fears over everyday tasks and things
- avoiding new or unusual situations
- feeling self-conscious or overly sensitive to criticism
- being irritable
- withdrawing from social activity
- having difficulty concentrating
- often struggling with headaches or stomach aches
- drop in school grades
- not wanting to go to school
- difficulty falling and staying asleep
- abusing substances

The exercises that we've discussed for evaluating your negative thoughts and regulating your emotions can be very effective in reducing your anxiety. I would encourage you to make notes of which exercises are most effective in helping you overcome your anxiety so that you can easily refer back to them during difficult times. Alternatively, here are two more exercises that have been specifically designed to help reduce anxiety: Find *Your Stop and Dive in Ice*.

Find Your Stop

If you often miss the signs of feeling anxious or practice mindfulness regularly, you may not even be aware of how intense your anxiety might be. This is where this exercise comes in. It's simply about using a visual cue that will remind you to stop and practice some relaxation exercises to help you calm down, ground yourself, consider your thoughts, validate your emotions, and decide what you want to do.

Think of a visual cue you can use. This can be a physical stop sign that you can print and post somewhere in your room or a physical artifact that you can pick up and hold whenever you need to cool off. I would recommend you create a couple of these "stop signs" or "stopping objects" that you can keep in places where you typically experience anxiety, such as in your bag that you keep in class with you, one to keep in your pocket, one where you do your homework, and next to your bed if you struggle with anxiety at night.

Every time you see your "stop sign" or feel it in your pocket, take a moment to pause.

Find a rhythm of deep breathing and then ask yourself some questions, such as:

- What am I thinking about?
- How am I feeling?
- What is upsetting me right now?
- How can I change my situation?
- What don't I have control over?
- What can I do next?

This technique will not only help you cope with your challenges; it will also help you become more aware of your anxiety and its symptoms.

Dive in Ice

This exercise may seem extremely unpleasant, but if you're willing to give it a try, you may just be amazed at the benefits you may gain by sitting in a bath full of ice-cold water or having a cold shower. These benefits include boosting your immune system and teaching yourself that you can act against your emotions: Even if everything within you tells you that you need to get out of the bath, you can practice mind-over-matter to stay in this cold water. You'll then even be able to resist the urge to act against your strong emotions and decide to do the opposite.

While it's most effective to submerge your body in a bath of cold water, you can do this gradually as well. For example, if you're in the shower, you can expose your body limb-by-limb to the cold water: first the one leg, then the other, then your one arm, and then your other. Continue doing this until your entire body has been exposed to the cold.

OVERCOMING DEPRESSION

Young children rely on their parents to jump in when they are feeling sad and either give them a literal shoulder to cry on or kiss their sores better. For teenagers, this can look a lot different. Your problems will become more complex, and you'll need more privacy in your life; talking to your parents about your difficulties won't be enough to console you.

If you're not paying attention to the anxiety or sadness that you may experience, this can easily lead to more serious conditions, one of which is depression. This mental health condition can put you on a slippery slope where you may lose interest in activities you used to enjoy, and it can get so severe that you start to consider suicide as your life might not seem worth living anymore.

Symptoms of depression you can look out for include:

- feeling irritable or sad most of the time
- struggling to concentrate
- feeling guilty over things that aren't your fault
- losing interest in the things you used to love doing
- feeling worthless
- changes to your sleeping or eating habits
- not having the energy or motivation to do anything
- losing hope in the future
- using substances to cope with your challenges
- having thoughts of hurting yourself or taking your own life

It's extremely important that you always keep an eye out for these signs of depression, and if you ever suspect that you might be depressed, talk to an adult immediately. This is a serious condition that will likely require the treatment and intervention of a doctor. Your doctor will talk to you about what you're feeling and experiencing. They may refer you to a psychologist for psychotherapy (such as CBT and DBT) or, in more severe cases, prescribe you medication in the form of antidepressants.

Since behavioral therapy forms part of the typical treatment of depression, don't disregard the power that the exercises in this book can have on your situation. Let's look at two more exercises that are very effective in reducing the impact of this mental health condition: Remember the Yets and Have a SEAT.

Remember the Yets

Depression often stems from struggling with your ability to do things or failing at tasks that you might believe should be easy to complete. When you start to doubt yourself and your own abilities, it can be difficult to bring yourself back to a good place and see the incredible value that you have within you. This is where the power of the word "yet" can change your life.

The next time you feel negative about your situation or your own abilities, add the word "yet" to your sentence. For example, instead of believing that you aren't a lovable person, you can turn this into a positive by saying, "I'm not a lovable person yet." Or, if you're struggling with math, you can create hope by saying, "I'm not good at math yet."

As you can see, this simple three-letter word can turn any potentially negative situation into a positive one filled with hope. You'll realize that you have the power within you to change your situation. Once you start to realize that there is hope in your situation, you can start to plan your next step and what you can do to turn this "yet" into a reality. Then, you can add the word "but" to your negative sentence to put your planning into action.

For example, you can say, "I'm not a lovable person yet, but if I show others more respect, this can change," or "I'm not good at math yet, but if I pay more attention in class and ask my teacher or tutor for help, I can learn to understand the math problems I'm struggling with." Suddenly, you'll know that you can overcome the difficulties that you face and have planned what your first step should be to turn your challenges into strengths.

Have a SEAT

The next exercise is built around the acronym SEAT and will help you evaluate the reality of your situation in a calm manner so that you can decide how you want to proceed. This will help you not only regulate your thoughts, emotions, and behavior but also make you realize that your situation may not be as bleak as you might have thought. It will help you get in touch with your reality and seek out the positives in your situation.

When you start with this exercise, it's best to do it in a quiet environment where you're comfortable and free from distractions. But, as you get used to becoming more mindful about your thoughts, emotions, and behavior, you'll be able to do this easily and in any situation.

Here's how to do this:

- **Sensation**: How are you feeling? Are you feeling tense? Do you have any pain? What can you see? What can you hear? What do you smell? What do you taste? What can you feel? To help you with this, you can do a quick self-soothing exercise to hone your senses or a muscle relaxation exercise to identify any pain in your body.
- **Emotions**: What emotions are you experiencing? Can you identify your primary and secondary emotions? What are the names of these emotions? Are you able to calm yourself down?
- **Actions**: How do you want to respond to your feelings? How would you want to react? Is there a difference between how you're currently behaving and how you would like to act? What are the potential consequences of your behavior? What can you do to respond more in line with your ideal behavior?
- **Thoughts**: What are you thinking about? Are these thoughts valid? What evidence is there to

support your thoughts? Are there any other ways in which you can view your situation? How would an outsider see your situation? What impact do your limiting beliefs have on your thoughts?

I would recommend that you add this exercise to your daily schedule and not just do it when you're feeling depressed or going through a difficult time. If you can turn this into a habit, you'll find yourself gradually becoming more grounded in yourself and your life.

When you experience difficulty in your life, you can choose to either let this get you down or to build yourself up to become the strongest version of yourself possible. In the next chapter, we'll look at how you can turn your adversities into opportunities to build resilience.

9

BUILDING RESILIENCE

On some days, it may feel like you're going from one challenge to the next, and on some days, it may even seem as if there's no way to overcome some of the challenges you may face. If you don't have the necessary resilience to bounce back after you're knocked down, you may find yourself struggling even more.

The good news is that you can build the necessary resilience to stand up no matter how many times life may knock you down. This will also help you to develop a growth mindset that can help you change the way you view your difficulties so that you can thrive in life and gain the confidence to build a trusting support system that can carry you through the bad days and celebrate with you on the good days.

CULTIVATING RESILIENCE

How badly do misfortunes affect you, even the most minor ones? How long do you struggle to get back to your tasks after you suffer a setback? Or, how difficult is it for you to accept the things you have no control over? Be honest with yourself when you answer these questions, as this will give you a good indication of your own resilience.

Being resilient means you'll be realistic when you look at the challenges you face, think rationally about your difficulties, and then find the silver lining in every situation so that you can push through regardless of how negative your situation may seem. Your resilience will help you make the best of your circumstances and put you in the right frame of mind to develop strategies that will help you thrive.

With every adversity you experience, you'll gain some resilience. Think of it as your body's internal muscle memory that remembers how you were able to overcome a challenge in the past and use these same techniques to deal with a similar struggle in the future. But you don't have to wait for your body to naturally build resilience; there are many different techniques you can use to gain the mental toughness you need to stand up no matter how many times your challenges knock you down.

This is similar to how you train your muscles to get stronger. Every time you move, your muscles develop, and the more you move and train specific muscles, the stronger you'll get physically. Your resilience can be viewed in the same way: The more you work on improving it, the stronger you'll get mentally.

Training your resilience is all about forcing your body to build tolerance for being uncomfortable. Just like the Dive in Ice exercise that we discussed in the previous chapter, these exercises are designed to teach you that you don't have to give in every time you're feeling uncomfortable and that you can act against your emotions.

Let's look at four exercises you can do to train your resilience:

- **Wait a few minutes**: When you're really hungry, all you'll want to do is eat a plate of your favorite food. While it's absolutely necessary to eat when you're hungry to fuel your body, waiting 10 minutes for your food won't affect your energy levels but can have amazing benefits in teaching you that you can overcome any discomfort you may experience. The next time you're really hungry, dish out a plate of food for yourself and put it on the table. Then, set a timer to go off after 10 minutes. Whenever your hunger pangs get too bad while you wait, remind yourself that it's okay to wait as you will eat soon. Once your timer goes off, you can pat yourself on the back for being able to wait and enjoy your meal.

- **Do something you dislike**: Keep your timer out for this exercise. If you have to do something you really dislike doing, set your timer for 10 minutes and force yourself to work on this task (and only this task) until your timer goes off. When your timer rings, you can choose whether you want to quit this task or continue with it to complete it. The chances are good that you'll continue working, as starting an unpleasant task is always the most difficult aspect of doing something you dislike. As simple as this exercise may seem, it will teach you that you don't have to respond to your emotions and that you can do something even if you lack the motivation to do it.
- **Switch off distractions**: Unless you enjoy doing physical exercise, you'll likely want some sort of distraction playing in the background, such as the TV, a podcast, or the radio, while

you work through your routine. While this can be very effective in ensuring that you get the physical exercise your body needs, you'll miss out on the opportunity for mental exercise. If you switch off all distractions while you're working out, you'll build tolerance for not only being uncomfortable but also pushing through with a task you don't enjoy.

- **Switch up the temperature**: When it's boiling hot, you'll likely want to switch the air conditioner to cool, and on a freezing day, you'll probably turn up the heat. To train your resilience, switch this around by either turning up the heat on a hot day and cooling the air conditioner on a cold day or switching off any form of temperature control altogether. You don't have to sit in this uncomfortable temperature for hours; about 10 to 20 minutes at a time may be enough for you to push through some discomfort.

- **Be grateful**: When you're going through a difficult time, it's easy to forget about all the good things in your life. You may focus so much on the negatives that you may not even recognize the many amazing things in your life, even if they're right in front of you. To help you overcome this, get into the habit of saying at least one thing a day that you're grateful for. Even if it's something as simple as having a warm bed to sleep in, saying it out loud will remind you that you have much more going right in your life than you may realize and that you shouldn't allow any obstacle you may face to get the better of you. Also, the more you become used to practicing gratitude, the easier it will be to find the silver lining in any situation.

The more you're able to overcome the discomfort in these exercises, the more you'll train your mind to believe that you can overcome even bigger discomforts and that the things that might have bothered you in the past won't be such a big obstacle anymore going forward.

CREATING A GROWTH MINDSET

As you're working on becoming more resilient, you may realize that your mindset might be holding you back. You may discover that you have a fixed mindset that makes it difficult for you to break free from and overcome the challenges you face. To help you with this, it's important that you work on developing a growth mindset.

These two terms, fixed and growth mindset, were developed by the renowned psychologist Carol Dweck and basically divide people's mindsets into two categories (Dweck, 2006):

Growth Mindset	Fixed Mindset
Embraces all challenges without fear.	Avoids challenges as much as possible.
Pushes through regardless of how many times you fail.	Gives up as soon as you reach the first major obstacle.
Believes that if you work hard at improving yourself, you can increase your skills and intelligence.	Believes that everyone was born with a specific level of intelligence and skills, and no matter what you do, this won't change.
Sees the success of others as an inspiration and source of motivation.	Is threatened by others who achieve more success than them.
Wants to learn and acknowledges that there's a lot they don't know.	Believes that they already know everything they'll ever need to know.
Accepts any form of feedback and criticism.	Avoids and even ignores any form of feedback.

Reading through the differences between these two mindsets, it may seem obvious that a growth mindset holds a lot more benefits than a fixed one. Still, many people struggle to adopt this positive mindset in their lives. Luckily, it's completely possible to develop a growth mindset. Seven steps you can take doing this include:

1. **Identify where you're currently at**: Before you can work on changing your mindset, you need to know which group you fall into. Read

through the list of traits of the two mindsets and determine where you're at.

2. **Define your reasons**: Why do you want to develop a growth mindset? What benefits do you think a growth mindset will bring to your life? What motivates you to make this change? The more clear you are on the reasons for making the change, the easier it will be to find motivation should you struggle on this journey.

3. **Look for examples**: Think about the people in your life. Who do you think has a growth mindset? Talk to them about their beliefs and how they adopted these mindsets. They might give you valuable insights that can help you on your journey. You can also ask them if they're willing to mentor you on this journey.

4. **Change how you view failure**: Start to think about failure as an opportunity to learn from your mistakes rather than seeing it as an inability to perform. Remind yourself that no one achieves anything in life without making some mistakes along the way. But the most successful people are able to learn from their failures.

5. **Know your abilities**: No matter what your goals may be, you may have limitations in your skill set that you need to be aware of. This will

help you not only identify what skills you need to work on to achieve success but also adjust your goals to make sure they are realistic and achievable.

6. **Take note of your thoughts about talent and skill**: You might find that you believe some people are simply naturally talented or that you just don't have the skills to do something. But if you change this line of thinking by actively looking at the amount of work the "naturally talented" person put into crafting their skill or adding the word "yet" when you think about your own shortcomings (as discussed in the previous chapter), you'll realize that you are capable of anything you set your mind to as long as you're willing to put in the hard work.

7. **Learn something everyday**: Try your best to learn something new daily. This can be something big that's connected to your schoolwork or something that interests you, or something as small as someone's name or phone number. The more you train your brain to remember things, the easier it will be to learn.

Once you've implemented these steps in your life, you should be well on your way to adopting a growth mindset. But, the work doesn't just end there. Now, you need to continue working on maintaining this mindset in your daily life. Actions you can consider to do this include:

- Seeing your challenges as positive opportunities rather than setbacks.
- Reflect daily on the mistakes you've made and what you can learn from them.
- Seeking only the approval of yourself, not others.
- Celebrate the success of others whenever you can, as this can be a valuable tool for motivation.

Acknowledging the hard work and successes of others will also help you build healthy relationships with others, which is a vital step in developing a proper support system.

DEVELOPING A SUPPORT SYSTEM

You've likely heard the well-known saying that there is safety in numbers many times before. This safety not only refers to your physical safety of having other people to protect you but also your emotional safety, where you have a support system that you can rely on in good times and bad.

While your support system may include teachers or other mentors, the most likely sources of support will come in the form of your family and friends. Let's first look at specific tips you can use to develop healthy relationships with your family:

- Show them love and appreciation, no matter how you might feel. Remember, your family members are only humans. They will also go through tough times and have difficult challenges to deal with.
- Try your best to eat together as a family and keep the TV off. If possible, sit together at a table and give everyone the opportunity to talk about their days and what's going on in their lives.
- Ask your parents if you can't go on a family outing together. Suggest that everyone in the family gets the chance to choose the activity you'll all do.
- Make an effort to spend one-on-one time with your family. This can even be as informal as talking to them while you're helping them with chores around the house or doing homework with a sibling.

- When family rules are discussed, ask for the opportunity to give your input as well. When you do this, don't disregard everything that your parents have said, but rather try to find a compromise that everyone is happy with.
- Request regular family meetings where any challenges can be discussed in a calm and loving manner.

Next, let's look at how you can find support in the form of friends. Firstly, decide how many friends you'd like to have. While some people prefer socializing in a large group, others prefer having only one or two close friends. Don't try to force yourself to have more or less of what you prefer; friendships should never be forced.

If you want to increase your friendship group but struggle to connect with others, these tips might be able to help:

- Think about your interests and how you can meet more people who share them. This might mean joining a specific social club or sports team.
- Spend time with family, friends, or extended family. You never know who you might meet at one of these gatherings.

- Pick one person you feel somewhat comfortable with and invite them to join you for an activity. Start with a relatively quick activity that doesn't necessarily require constant conversation. If this goes well, you can always arrange to meet up again.
- Invite a friend over to your house (your comfort zone) and ask your family to give you some privacy (and lock any embarrassing photo albums away).
- Consider volunteering at a community project. This can be another fantastic way of meeting other people with similar interests to yours.

The skills you've learned in this book won't mean anything if you don't know how to effectively implement them in your life by setting proper goals and making sure you maintain progress. In the next chapter, we'll discuss putting it all together to help you become the best possible version of yourself.

10

PUTTING IT ALL TOGETHER

Many people make the mistake of expecting others to bring them happiness while they sit back and do nothing to seek out the things they want from life. We all have dreams for our lives and things we hope to one day achieve, but what are you actually doing to make these dreams a reality?

Your life is in your hands, and instead of simply sitting back and thinking about what you want to achieve while you hope others will make it happen for you, you should start to plan what you can do to achieve your goals. While this may seem fairly simple, too many people never reach their desired outcomes, often not because they're lazy or incapable but because they just don't know where to start or struggle to overcome their negative thoughts, limiting beliefs, and intense emotions.

If you continue working on yourself and making use of the exercises in this book, you'll soon be able to master the mind-body connection that may have been holding you back. Then, you'll only need to work on proper planning so that you can make sure you stay on the right path to reach your goals.

CREATING A PERSONALIZED PLAN

When you create a personalized plan for your life, you're essentially developing a roadmap or guide that will help you turn your dreams into reality. Apart from this, it will also help you to feel more in control of your life and make better decisions, as these choices will be based on getting you closer to your outcomes.

It's important that you make sure this plan remains flexible; you should never allow a rigid plan to control your life. You always have to keep space for unforeseen possibilities or crises, as these will inevitably pop up in your life. Let's look at the steps you can follow to create your own personalized plan:

- **Identify your vision**: Start by visualizing your dream life and try to include as much detail as you can, such as what you're doing, how you're feeling, and who you have in your life. Make notes of your vision or create your own vision board of what your dream life looks like.

- **Assess your life**: Next, take stock of the various aspects of your life, such as your relationships, health, or personal growth. What aspects require the most work? What mistakes have you made in the past? What lessons can you learn from your past failures? What strengths do you have? How can you use your strengths more to improve your life?
- **Prioritize your life**: Once you know which aspects you need to work on, list them according to their urgency and the impact they will have on your life. Once you've prioritized your list, decide whether the least important points on it really deserve your attention or if they may just waste your time. While reading through your list, you might realize that your unimportant tasks don't deserve a place on it at all.
- **Create an action plan**: Decide which tasks on your list you want to take on first and what steps you need to take to reach your desired outcomes. This will include setting proper goals for yourself, something we'll discuss in the next

section.
- **Adjust where you have to**: No plan can ever be set in stone. There will always be aspects that require adjustment, whether this is your plan, your goal, or your desired outcome. Make time to review your action plan so that you can make the necessary adjustments as and when they become necessary.

Most importantly, never give up on your dreams and hopes for the future. There will be obstacles on your journey, but if you're able to push past them, you can have the life you've always wanted.

SETTING GOALS

Goals will help you plan your tasks so that you can reach the outcomes that you want in your life. It's about taking your priority list and then deciding on specific steps you need to take so that you can tick off tasks on your list. This sounds simple enough, doesn't it? Yes, the simple act of setting goals is easy. But making sure these goals are realistic and achievable isn't always as simple as it may seem.

You've probably heard of SMART goals before. There's a reason why these types of goals are so popular; this acronym will help you make sure your goals are specific, measurable, achievable, realistic, and time-bound. Let's look at what this means:

- **Specific**: You need to know exactly what you want to achieve and what you're going to do to reach this goal.
- **Measurable**: You need to be able to measure the progress that you make to achieve your goals, as this will help you to witness how your life is improving. Seeing your success will also help motivate you to work even harder at reaching even more goals.
- **Achievable**: You have to make sure that your goals are within your reach. It can demotivate you if the goals seem too far away or difficult to achieve. When this is the case, you can chunk your goals into smaller tasks that are easier to achieve.
- **Realistic**: Your goals should always fit in with your skills and capabilities. If you set goals that are too difficult, you'll set yourself up for failure. Similarly, if your goals are too easy, you may get bored and give up. Make sure that your goals are possible, interesting, and important enough to keep your attention.

- **Time-bound**: You need to set yourself deadlines for when you want to achieve your goals. This will help you be more accountable and plan the various tasks you may have to complete.

Let's look at an example of how you can set a SMART goal. Let's say your goal is to get an A for your next science assignment. First, you need to define the reasons why you didn't get your desired grade for your previous assignment. Identifying the mistakes from your past will help you know exactly what you need to work on improving in the future. Then, use this template to define your goal:

My primary goal:	To get an A on my next science assignment.
My previous mistakes:	I procrastinated on my previous assignment. This meant that I didn't have enough time to complete the necessary research for my assignment or double-check it for errors. I also lost marks by handing in my assignment late.
My chunked-down goals:	<ul><li>I will start my next assignment immediately after I get it.</li><li>I will give myself three days to do my research and another two days to complete the assignment.</li><li>I will ask my mom to proofread the assignment for mistakes.</li></ul>
What and when:	If I get my assignment on Monday and have a week to complete it, my timing will be as follows:<ul><li>I will start my research on Monday and make sure it's completed by Wednesday night.</li><li>I will complete my assignment on Thursday and Friday.</li><li>On Saturday, I will give my assignments to mom to check for any mistakes.</li><li>On Sunday, I will fix any mistakes that mom might find and go through it one last time to make sure it's ready.</li><li>Next Monday, I will hand in my assignment on time.</li></ul>

Making sure your goals fulfill these criteria may seem like a time-consuming process, but the more effort you put into defining your goals, the better the chances will be of you reaching your outcomes. It will be well worth your time to clearly define your steps.

Always make sure your goals are written down. This will also help to ensure that you always know what your next step should be and can give you something to refer back to when you have to make important decisions. If you're a visual learner, it can be helpful to include pictures when you make notes of your goals, as this will keep you motivated to reach your dreams.

In the example above, you asked your mom to help check your assignment for mistakes. In doing this, she became your accountability partner, or simply put, your goal buddy. This is someone that you either include in your goal or talk about your goal so that they can help you reach your outcome.

When you identify your goal buddy, you need to ask them if they're willing to become involved in your goal and to what extent they are willing to help you. Then, depending on their level of involvement, you can ask them to do regular check-ins to make sure you stay on track to reach your goals or to help you find solutions to any problems you may face along the way.

MAINTAINING PROGRESS

As you start seeing the results of implementing these CBT and DBT skills into your life, you will likely be more motivated than ever before to continue with your good work to improve your life. But, no matter how good you may start to feel about what you've already achieved, remind yourself that this is just the start of your journey. Now, you'll have to stay committed to the process so that you can reap even more rewards.

Maintaining the progress, you've already made means you need to continue to practice these exercises repeatedly so that you can progress and improve even more. Think of this as learning to play a new musical instrument, for example, the piano. When you start playing the piano, you first need to learn to identify the various keys and how to read music. Then, you'll be taught to play your first few notes. This might feel like a triumph, but if you don't continue to practice and push yourself to play more notes, you will never become a master pianist. Many people will give up after learning to play their first basic song, while only a few will excel.

The same goes for working at improving your life by managing your emotions and challenging your negative thoughts. You will achieve some level of success after the first while incorporating CBT and DBT into your life. But to truly become a master of your own emotions and thoughts and improve all aspects of your life, you need to continue with your efforts.

If you encounter any obstacles that might hamper your progress, you can do a quick grounding session to help you become more mindful in the present moment. We've already discussed many grounding and relaxation techniques that you can use to find calm in even the most difficult circumstances. Another technique you can use is called the 5-4-3-2-1 coping strategy.

This technique is extremely simple but very effective. Since you only need your senses to do this exercise, you can do it anywhere. Start by finding a deep breathing pattern, then follow these easy steps by seeking out:

- five things you can see
- four things you can touch
- three things you can hear
- two things you can touch
- one thing you can taste

The increase in self-awareness and mindfulness will help you refocus on your reality and what's really happening in your immediate environment. When you do this regularly, you'll soon become a master of becoming calm and more mindful. This will also help you use the techniques you've learned in this book as you transition into adulthood, which we'll discuss in the last chapter.

11

LOOKING AHEAD

Life can get crazy busy. You're likely inundated with school projects, sporting commitments, and cultural activities. In between that, you need to make time for your family and social life, and work on improving yourself using the exercises in this book. This can easily result in you forgetting to celebrate the wins that you gain along the way.

As you follow this journey, always make sure you give yourself credit when it's due. When you practice mindfulness, focus on what you have achieved as well as how you're feeling. Pay attention to the small accomplishments as well as the big ones, as any success, no matter how small it may seem, adds up to bring self-mastery to your life.

CELEBRATE YOUR PROGRESS

When you celebrate your various wins, you'll boost not only your motivation but also your self-esteem. You'll remind yourself of the greatness that you're capable of and that you can not only reach your goals, but you can also learn to have fun doing so. Let's look at different ways you can celebrate your progress:

- **Create a mantra**: Something as simple as a celebratory mantra can often be enough to help you notice your successes and boost your confidence. This can be something such as, "I am becoming my best self," "I'm awesome," or "I'm creating a fantastic future for myself."
- **Have a fun day**: Celebrate your progress by having fun doing something you really enjoy.
- **Brag about your success**: When you achieve a win, you're allowed to brag about yourself, especially if you've done something you've struggled with in the past. If you belong to any family or social texting groups, share your good news there. Or, if you feel too shy to share your good news yourself, ask someone else in the group to send the message on your behalf.
- **Treat yourself to something sweet**: Whether this is a small cookie, an elaborate cake, or a

fancy dessert, ask your parents for the ingredients and bake it yourself. Creating this sweet treat by yourself will give you another reason to celebrate.
- **Create a playlist**: If you enjoy music, consider creating a celebratory playlist that you'll only listen to once you've reached a goal. This will also help to motivate you to push through your tasks to get your reward.
- **Do something new**: There might be something that you've always wanted to try but never did. Do this as your reward for completing your goal.

DEVELOP LIFELONG SKILLS

While working on improving your current life and managing your intense emotions more effectively, it's important that you also look to the future. The thought of becoming an adult can be extremely scary. While the DBT and CBT techniques discussed in this book will help you cope with your intense emotions over adulthood more effectively, you can also start to adopt some skills that will help you prepare for the transition into becoming an adult.

Go through the skills I've listed below and decide which one you want to work on adopting into your life first. There might even be some skills that you already have, so tick them off your list and continue to practice them on a daily basis. Let's look at the skills all teenagers should be able to do:

- **Consider getting a part-time job**: This can be very helpful in identifying the things that you enjoy doing and the strengths you might have that you may not even be aware of. Think about the things that you're really interested in or enjoy doing. How can you turn this into a part-time job? If you can turn this into something where you can earn pocket money, it will be a bonus. Otherwise, consider volunteering or shadowing someone to gain experience. The insights you can gain by doing this will be invaluable in narrowing your options for when you have to make decisions on what to study or what line of work to go into once you're done with school.
- **Start your financial management**: When you ask adults about their biggest causes of concern, most of them will say finances. As a teenager, you need to rely on either the pocket money your parents or guardians give you or the money you make from working part-time. This gives you the perfect opportunity to start

experimenting with budgeting and creating good spending and saving habits. To create a budget, you can either set up a spreadsheet on a computer or even just use a sheet of paper that you draw columns on. I would suggest you start out with the following categories:

- **Income**: If you have a set income per month or week, you can add this here. But if you earn a different amount every month, look at your earnings over the past six months and add the lowest income to your budget.
- **Necessary expenses**: These are the bills you have every month, such as your phone bills or whatever else you have to pay for.
- **Savings**: In an ideal world, you should try to save between 20–30% of your monthly income. So, if you earn $100 per month, you need to try to save between $20 and $30 every month.
- **Extra expenses**: These are your budget for entertainment or other nice-to-haves that you may choose to spend your money on. Try to keep this to at most 30% of your income.
- **Learn to cook**: It's important that you learn to prepare at least two or three basic meals. You might think now that you'll be able to eat out daily, but once you need to pay for this yourself, you may be shocked at how expensive and

unhealthy this is. Think about the food that you really enjoy eating, and then ask your parents if they can teach you how to make it. Don't think of extravagant meals. Learn to prepare food that is affordable and easy to make.

- **Start new cleaning habits**: Once you move out of your childhood home, all household chores will become your own responsibility. You may already have some cleaning habits when it comes to your own room, but how often do you help out with bigger cleaning tasks, such as doing laundry and washing the toilets? Start with simple habits, such as making your bed every day, packing away your own laundry, washing the dishes, spending 10 minutes every night picking up things that are out of place and clean, and decluttering your spaces regularly.
- **Consider your online presence**: It's important to think about how future bosses will view your online presence. Most employers look at the social media accounts of potential future employees before they hire them, so start to consider cleaning your accounts by untagging yourself in posts you don't want to be associated with and thinking twice before you post things. You can also consider setting up an

"adult" email account where you use only your name or initials as an email handle.

Don't allow yourself to be overwhelmed by your preparations for adulthood. Take it one step at a time, and before you know it, you may be ready for anything life may bring.

CONCLUSION

You now have all the skills you need to help you manage the struggles that come with adolescence more effectively, including regulating your emotions, controlling your negative thoughts, and limiting beliefs, and choosing to behave in helpful ways. You also have a better understanding of your own challenges and how your brain's development and increase in hormone levels can affect your daily life.

You realize the positive impact of behavioral therapy, such as CBT's cognitive distortions, by focusing on DBT's four pillars, namely mindfulness, interpersonal effectiveness, distress tolerance, and emotional regulation. What's more, you also understand the impact that the mind-body connection can have on how you respond to events and know that your physical health can have a major impact on your mental and emotional wellness as well.

Now that you have all these tools at your disposal, it's up to you to use them and become the best version of yourself. You can have the relationships with others that you so deeply want. You can remove explosive emotions and behaviors from your life. And, you can find the happiness you deserve.

Go out there, use your new tools, and create the life that you've always desired.

If you enjoyed the book and found the exercises and tips provided valuable in managing the various challenges you face on a daily basis, help me assist others as well by leaving a review on Amazon.

REFERENCES

Any anxiety disorder. (n.d.). National Institute of Mental Health. https://www.nimh.nih.gov/health/statistics/any-anxiety-disorder

Carroll, D. W. (2019, September 4). *The relationship between thoughts, feelings and behaviors.* Debbie Woodall Carroll, LPCC-S. https://debbiewoodallcarroll.com/the-relationship-between-thoughts-feelings-and-behaviors/

Check the facts. (n.d.). DBT Self Help. https://dbtselfhelp.com/dbt-skills-list/emotion-regulation/check-the-facts/

Cherry, K. (2022, August 10). *Cognitive behavioral therapy.* Verywell Mind. https://www.verywellmind.com/what-is-cognitive-behavior-therapy-2795747

Cherry, K. (2023, April 7). *How behavioral therapy is used in psychology.* Verywell Mind. https://www.verywellmind.com/what-is-behavioral-therapy-2795998

Cleare, A. (n.d.). *Weird and wonderful facts about teenagers.* Positive Parenting Project. https://anitacleare.co.uk/weird-wonderful-facts-teenagers/

Compitus, K. (2020, October 1). *What are distress tolerance skills? Your ultimate DBT toolkit.* Positive Psychology. https://positivepsychology.com/distress-tolerance-skills/

Cronkleton, E. (2019, April 9). *10 breathing techniques for stress relief and more.* Healthline. https://www.healthline.com/health/breathing-exercise

Cuncic, A. (2023, February 23). *How to change your negative thought patterns when you have SAD.* Verywell Mind. https://www.verywellmind.com/how-to-change-negative-thinking-3024843

Dowd, S. (2023, January 25). *What to do if you think your teenager is depressed.* Child Mind Institute. https://childmind.org/article/how-to-help-your-depressed-teenager/

Dweck, C. (2006). *Mindset: How You Can Fulfil Your Potential.* Robinson.

Eatough, E. (2021, June 10). *How to create a life plan.* BetterUp. https://www.betterup.com/blog/life-planning

Emotion regulation. (n.d.). DBT Self Help. https://dbt-selfhelp.com/dbt-skills-list/ emotion-regulation/

Exercise and mental health. (2023, May 24). Health Direct. https://www.healthdirect.gov.au/exercise-and-mental-health

Ferguson, S. (2022, December 20). *How to practice STOP mindfulness.* Psych Central. https://psychcentral.com/health/4-quick-mindfulness-techniques

Gordon, S. (2021, July 26). *What teens needs to know about setting boundaries.* Verywell Family. https://www.verywellfamily.com/boundaries-what-every-teen- needs-to-know-5119428

Healthy eating during adolescence. (2015). Johns Hopkins Medicine. https://www.hopkinsmedicine.org/health/wellness-and-prevention/healthy-eating-during-adolescence

Helping students connect the dots: Thoughts, feelings, and behaviors. (n.d.). Classroom Mental Health. https://classroommentalhealth.org/in-class/thoughts/

How to get people to do what you want using DBT skills. (2021, September 8). Discovery Ranch.

https://www.discoveryranch.net/dbt-skill-dear-man/

Hutto, C. (n.d.). *14 creative ways to celebrate small wins.* In Her Sight. https://www.inhersight.com/blog/career-development/celebrate-small-wins

Jacobson, R. (2023, January 5). *Teens and anger.* Child Mind Institute. https://childmind.org/article/teens-and-anger/

Jones, H. (2022, March 25). *What is the ABC model for cognitive therapy?* Verywell Health. https://www.verywellhealth.com/abc-therapy-5217670

Linehan, M. (n.d.). *Emotional regulation skills.* DBT Tools. https://dbt.tools/emotional_regulation/index.php

Miller, C. (2023, January 5). *How anxiety affects teenagers.* Child Mind Institute. https://childmind.org/article/signs-of-anxiety-in-teenagers/

Moods: helping pre-teens and teens manage emotional ups and downs. (n.d.). Raising Children Network. https://raisingchildren.net.au/pre-teens/mental-health- physical-health/about-mental-health/ups-downs

Morin, A. (2022, November 30). *11 ways to calm yourself fast when you're really mad.* Verywell Mind. https://www.verywellmind.com/anger-management-strategies- 4178870

Nariman, J. (2021, January 4). *How to help teens set effective goals (tips & templates)*. Big Life Journal. https://biglifejournal.com/blogs/blog/guide-effective-goal- setting-teens-template-worksheet

Peterson, T. J. (2023, August 10). *Progressive muscle relaxation: How it works, benefits, and tips*. Choosing Therapy. https://www.choosingtherapy.com/ progressive-muscle-relaxation/

Physical activity for older children and teenagers. (2018, March 19). Raising Children Network. https://raisingchildren.net.au/teens/healthy-lifestyle/physical-activity/physical-activity-teens

Quinn, D. (2021, August 30). *Mind-body connection: How it impacts substance use and mental health*. Sandstone Care. https://www.sandstonecare.com/blog/ mind-body-connection-10-facts-impacts-substance-use-mental-health/

Raypole, C. (2023, March 27). *9 ways to kick off your self-discovery journey*. Healthline. https://www.healthline.-com/health/self-discovery

Relationships with parents and families: why teenagers need them. (2021, November 29). Raising Children Network. https://raisingchildren.net.au/pre-teens/ communicating-relationships/family-relationships/relationships-with-parents-teens

Resilience in teenagers: how to build it. (2021, July 12). Raising Children Network. https://raisingchildren.net.au/pre-teens/development/social-emotional-development/resilience-in-teens

Schimelpfening, N. (2023, May 1). *What to know about dialectical behavior therapy.* Verywell Mind. https://www.verywellmind.com/dialectical-behavior-therapy-1067402

Schneiderman, M. (2023, January 5). *10 mental toughness exercises to help you become more resilient.* Fatherly. https://www.fatherly.com/life/mental-toughness-exercises

Scott, E. (2022, December 1). *What is mindfulness?* Verywell Mind. https://www.verywellmind.com/mindfulness-the-health-and-stress-relief-benefits-3145189

Teach your teenager to be resilient. (n.d.). ReachOut. https://parents.au.reachout.com/skills-to-build/wellbeing/things-to-try-coping-skills-and-resilience/teach-your-teenager-to-be-resilient

Teenage friends and friendships. (2021, September 13). Raising Children Network. https://raisingchildren.net.au/pre-teens/behaviour/peers-friends-trends/teen-friendships

Teenagers and communication. (2014, August 21). Better Health Channel. https://www.betterhealth.vic.gov.au/health/healthyliving/teenagers-and-communication

Teenagers and sleep. (2018, November 5). Better Health Channel; Better health channel. https://www.betterhealth.vic.gov.au/health/healthyliving/teenagers-and-sleep

The importance of goal-setting for teens. (2022, January 19). Boys and Girls Club of America. https://www.bgca.org/news-stories/2022/January/the-importance-of-goal-setting-for-teens

Understanding your emotions (for teens). (n.d.). Nemours Teen Health. https://kidshealth.org/en/teens/understand-emotions.html

Vivyan, C. (2009). *What now?* https://www.getselfhelp.co.uk/docs/EndingTherapy.pdf

Watson, S. (2020, January 7). *Relapse prevention plan: Techniques to help you stay on track.* Healthline. https://www.healthline.com/health/opioid-withdrawal/relapse-prevention-plan

Wooll, M. (2021, July 26). *A growth mindset is a must-have — these 13 tips will grow yours.* Betterup. https://www.betterup.com/blog/growth-mindset

Printed in Great Britain
by Amazon